HANDFULS ON PURPOSE

MICHAEL VIDAURRI, D. MIN.

AUTHOR'S NOTE: Some names of persons mentioned in this book have been changed to protect privacy; any similarity between individuals described in this book to individuals known to readers is purely coincidental.

Foreword

God's Word is a lifeline, a life changer, and a life saver! I know because it has been all that, and so much more for me personally!

In May, 1984 I was in my mid-thirties, struggling with severe panic/anxiety disorder causing numerous attacks every single day, night-terrors to the point of extreme sleep deprivation which caused difficulty concentrating, which of course also caused problems at work! PLUS, the panic/anxiety was quickly turning into agoraphobia. That caused even more fear, stress and physical illness because I was the sole parent of two young children and what would we do if I couldn't work? Honestly, I was at the point of total breakdown and death—I couldn't take it anymore! I had hit the bottom and had no family to turn to for help. As a matter of fact my problems had started as a result of my horribly neglectful, mentally/emotionally abusive family probably the minute I was born! Both sides of my family were mentally and emotionally crippled. I don't remember anyone ever laughing, having fun, being gentle or loving, but I do remember the ugliness, the sarcasm, the loneliness, the disdain, and the uncertainty— I was taught to fear everything!

In the middle of that dark night in May, 1984, I cried out to God for help—if not for me, at least for my two, innocent children— they had no one else to care for them! I begged Him to show me what to do to get out of the situation I was in—to change my life. I didn't know God, didn't know anything about His Word and didn't know if He'd heard me, or even cared that I was hanging on to life by my fingernails. All I'd ever heard was "God can do anything He wants to do—BUT, it might not be His Will to answer certain people, or certain prayers, because maybe He wants some people to suffer!"

I kept crying hysterically—I couldn't stop. I couldn't sleep, and I was SOOOOO exhausted and of course, had to work the next day. I didn't even know if I was going to make it to the morning! After a while, I felt like I was being directed to find my Bible. Why? I didn't know, but I began to search and found it dusty, and untouched, in the bottom of a drawer. I took it out and just held it for a few minutes, still sobbing and wiping away the torrential stream of tears. Then, I felt like I was being directed to open it—I don't mean I heard anything audible, just an impression from deep within. But open it to where?! If someone had said open it to 2nd John, or 1st Samuel, etc., I would have had no idea where any of those were located. So I just let it fall open on my lap. I looked down and the first thing my eyes focused on was the scripture: "I have heard your cries and seen your tears and I will heal you" (2 Kings 20:5). I was STUNNED. I knew that was specifically meant for me! I didn't know why, how or when, BUT God had heard me and answered.

That was the beginning of my healing and my life transformation but it didn't happen overnight. I started to church. Pastors, church counselors, and members I consulted with in regard to the extreme fear I battled would say in very religious tones things like: "perfect love casts out fear." I knew that was a scripture but what did it mean? Did it mean I had to somehow figure out how to become "perfect" in love? How does an imperfect person become perfect in anything? Did it mean God has "perfect love" and I had to find a way to get Him to give it to me? What exactly was perfect love? Where and how did I get it so I could get rid of the fear? Nobody could explain that to me! Finally, I realized I was going to have to dig into the Bible myself and learn who God was, what He expected of me, and how to live out His will. So I began that journey. I started reading the Bible daily, listening to tapes by Pastors like Kenneth Copeland, Jerry

Savelle, and others. I heard the scripture "For God hath not given me the spirit of fear (make no mistake fear IS a spirit!), but of power, of love and of a sound mind. Now that was a shocker! If God hadn't given me the spirit of fear where had it come from? I found the scripture that answered that question succinctly and quickly: "For he (Satan) comes but for to steal, kill, and destroy." Satan was trying to steal the life God had given me. Then I read the rest of that verse: "but I (Jesus) came to give you life and that more abundantly") That did it! God was on MY side and Satan had to go! But how did I make him flee?

I kept studying and found the scriptures "My son (male and females alike) attend to My words; incline your ear to my sayings. Let them not depart from before your eyes; keep them in the midst of your heart. For they are life to all of them who find them, and health to all their flesh. Keep your heart with all diligence; for out of it flow the issues of life." (See Proverbs 4:20-23). And Proverbs 18:20-21, which says, "Life and death are in the power of the tongue."

And that's where Pastor Mike came in. He broke down those scriptures for me, and so many more, so that I could understand exactly what they meant and how to use them DAILY to defeat the wiles of the enemy. When I knew how to put it to work, The Word began to work like nothing I'd ever experienced! God healed me completely of panic/anxiety and agoraphobia and I had battled that for over twenty years. God healed me of physical problems. He taught me how to forgive those who'd hurt me, and forgave me for hurting others. He promised He would "restore the years the locusts had eaten" and He has been faithful—I have been able to realize my lifelong dream (since the age of eight) of becoming an author with four highly praised books now in print, and one due out next year.

I can't say enough great things about Pastor Mike. He is absolutely a man of God. He has devoted his life to studying, learning, explaining, and living the Word of God. He digs into the Greek and Hebrew languages in order to break down the scriptures so that ANYONE can understand the scriptures. I have learned so much from him and it has absolutely changed my life. Your life will be changed for the better as well, if you will begin digging into the Word daily— start with ten minutes, more if you can.

And while you're doing that, read Handfuls on Purpose. It has a scripture and message for each day of the month. At the end of each devotion there is a confession that you need to not only read, but **SAY OUT LOUD** several times a day. There are many scriptures in the Bible about how powerful the words are that come out of your mouth. E.g. Your world is framed by the words of your mouth (See Hebrews 11:3), and Mark 11:24 where Jesus says, "Therefore I tell you whatever things you ask for **WHEN YOU PRAY, BELIEVE** that you receive them, and you will have them."

And remember "Jesus is the HIGH PRIEST of our confession". What is our "confession"? It is whatever you are ALLOWING to come out of your mouth! If you are saying things like "Oh, this job is killing me" or "That just scared me to death!" STOP IT!!!! Watch your mouth! Don't send invitations to the enemy to get a toe-hold in your life.

Pastor Mike can help with that and he LOVES to do it. He has several books coming out this year, all devoted to assist in the understanding and the DO-ING of the Word of God.

Linda Horton
Author of **TIME & AGAIN, TIME WILL TELL, FEAR NOT, EVERYDAY BLESSINGS and MIRACLES: True Stories of Godly Miracles, Large & Small**, and soon to be released: **ONLY BELIEVE**.
For more information see www.lindahorton.com

Introduction

In Romans 10:17 we are told that faith comes from hearing the Word of God. It is not only the hearing of the Word preach by a minister that ushers in faith, but it is the hearing and then receiving revelation knowledge about who we are and what we have access to in Jesus, that produces faith in the Believer. I have written these thirty-one daily devotions for that purpose.

I pray that as you read and re-read these devotions that you will begin to hear and understand the truth about who you are IN CHRIST. I pray that they encourage your spirit (the real YOU), and that they Bless your soul. It is my hope that as a result of reading these devotions you are spurred onward to discover all of the great and precious promises that our Heavenly Father has given to each and every one of us who belong to Him through faith in Jesus.

Grab a hold of the truth that God is for you, that He loves you, and wants you to succeed and flourish in His BLESSING! Jesus said about Himself in John 10:10 (AMP), "I came that they may have and enjoy life, and have it in abundance (to the full, till it overflows)."

I believe that as you read these devotions God's Word will radically change your life. I hope that they give you the desire to begin making daily confessions over your life, family, career, finances, and everything else that concerns you. As you do, I pray that you experience the TRUE BIBLICAL SUCCESS that Joshua 1:8 (AMP) promises. "This Book of the Law shall not depart out of your mouth, but you shall meditate on it day and night, that you may observe and do according to all that is written in it. For then you shall make your way prosperous, and then you shall deal wisely and have good success."

Table of Contents

Day 1

Handfuls On Purpose

"^{10} Then she fell on her face, bowing to the ground, and said to him, Why have I found favor in your eyes that you should notice me, when I am a foreigner? ^{11} And Boaz said to her, I have been made fully aware of all you have done for your mother-in-law since the death of your husband, and how you have left your father and mother and the land of your birth and have come to a people unknown to you before. ^{12} The Lord recompense you for what you have done, and a full reward be given you by the Lord, the God of Israel, under Whose wings you have come to take refuge! ^{13} Then she said, Let me find favor in your sight, my lord. For you have comforted me and have spoken to the heart of your maidservant, though I am not as one of your maidservants. ^{14} And at mealtime Boaz said to her, Come here and eat of the bread and dip your morsel in the sour wine [mixed with oil]. And she sat beside the reapers; and he passed her some parched grain, and she ate until she was satisfied and she had some left [for Naomi]. ^{15} And when she got up to glean, Boaz ordered his young men, Let her glean even among the sheaves, and do not reproach her. ^{16} *And let fall some handfuls for her on purpose and let them lie there for her to glean, and do not rebuke her.*" (Emphasis Added).

Ruth 2:10-16 (AMP)

The story of Ruth and Boaz is very similar to the story of Jesus and the Body of Christ. Boaz was a kinsman redeemer and Jesus is our Savior and Redeemer from sin, sickness, and all of the effects of the Curse.

In Ruth 2:1 we read, "Now Naomi had *a kinsman* of her husband's, a man of wealth, of the family of Elimelech, whose name was Boaz." In Ruth 3:9 (NIV) we read about an interaction which takes place between Boaz and Ruth, "Who are you?" he asked. "I am your servant Ruth," she said. "Spread the corner of your garment over me, since *you are a guardian-redeemer* of our family." The Amplified Bible renders the verse this way, "And he said, Who are you? And she answered, I am Ruth your maidservant. *Spread your wing [of protection] over your maidservant*, for you are a next of kin."

I want you to understand that according to Romans 8:16-17, Jesus is our Kinsman (our close relative) who sticks closer than a brother (See Proverbs 18:24), and our Guardian-Redeemer. Paul wrote of Him, "The Spirit Himself bears witness with our spirit that we are children of God, [17] and if children, then heirs—heirs of God and joint heirs with Christ." In other words, because we are both children of God and joint heirs with Jesus, you and I have legal access to *ALL* that our Heavenly Father has.

That means that all that He has, has already been freely given to us, so we don't need to beg Him for it. All we need to do is to ask Him and He will gladly give it to us. Matthew 7:7-11 says, "[7] Ask, and it will be given to you; seek, and you will find; knock, and it will be opened to you. [8] For everyone who asks receives, and he who seeks finds, and to him who knocks it will be opened. [9] Or what man is there among you who, if his son asks for bread, will give him a stone? [10] Or if he asks for a fish, will he give him a serpent? [11] If you then, being evil, know how to give good gifts to your children, how much more will your Father who is in heaven give good things to those who ask Him!" God wants to give you all the good things that you can handle, all of the good things that you both need and desire.

Now look with me at Galatians 3:13-14, 29. Here, Paul writes about Jesus saying, "[13] Christ has redeemed us from the curse of the law, having become a curse for us...[14] that the blessing of Abraham might come upon the Gentiles in Christ Jesus, that we might receive the promise of the Spirit through faith...[29] And if you are Christ's, then you are Abraham's seed, and heirs according to the promise." God has redeemed us from EVERY symptom of the Curse in Christ. If we are redeemed from it, then we shouldn't put up with it—redemption is deliverance from a thing.

Think about the similarities between the relationship that Boaz and Ruth shared and the relationship that we share with Jesus. Ruth was a foreigner living in the land of her deceased husband. She was living there caring for her mother-in-law who had no other support or immediate family. As Believers we are living in a foreign land too. In John 17:14-18 Jesus prays to the Father saying, "[14] I have given them Your word; and the world has hated them *because they are not of the world*, just as I am not of the world. [15] I do not pray that You should take them out of the world, but that You should keep them from the evil one. [16] *They are not of the world, just as I am not of the world.* [17] Sanctify them by Your truth. Your word is truth. [18] As You sent Me into the world, I also have sent them into the world." (Emphasis Added).

We are not of this world. We are foreigners in a strange land—a sin infected land. Even though humanity has been contaminated by the sin of our spiritual parents Adam and Eve, sin was never God's purpose for us. His purpose was for us to enjoy and to thrive in the Blessing. The Blessing is comprised of complete goodness, wholeness, and love. The Blessing has no bad side effects. Proverbs 10:22 states, "The blessing of the Lord makes one rich, and He adds no sorrow with it." Ephesians 1:3 says, "[3] Blessed be the God and Father of our Lord Jesus Christ, who has blessed us with every spiritual blessing in the heavenly places in Christ."

John writes in 3 John 2, "Beloved, I pray that you may prosper in all things and be in health, just as your soul prospers." If we go back to Genesis 12:1-2, and to the Blessing that God originally pronounced over Abraham, we find, "Now the Lord had said to Abram: "Get out of your country, from your family and from your father's house, to a land that I will show you. [2] I will make you a great nation; I will bless you and make your name great; and you shall be a blessing."

In 2 Corinthians 8:9 we read, "For you know the grace of our Lord Jesus Christ, that though He was rich, yet for your sakes He became poor, that you through His poverty might become rich."

In 2 Corinthians 9:8-12 we find, "[8] And God is able to make all grace abound toward you, that you, always having all sufficiency in all things, may have an abundance for every good work. [9] As it is written: "He has dispersed abroad, He has given to the poor; His righteousness endures forever." [10] Now may He who supplies seed to the sower, and bread for food, supply and multiply the seed you have sown and increase the fruits of your righteousness, [11] while you are enriched in everything for all liberality, which causes thanksgiving through us to God. [12] For the administration of this service not only supplies the needs of the saints, but also is abounding through many thanksgivings to God."

In every single one of these instances, God is doing something GOOD, for His covenant Children. He is being a Blessing to him or her and illustrating His love for them. I want you to know and understand that it is God's will for you to live BLESSED and to live

WHOLE in every area of your life! God wants you Blessed in your spirit, Blessed in your soul: your mind, your will, and your emotions. He wants you Blessed in your body and free from all sickness, disease, and discomfort. And God also wants you Blessed in your finances, Blessed in your relationships, and Blessed in all that you put your hand to. Deuteronomy 28:8 says, "The Lord will command the blessing on you in your storehouses and in all to which you set your hand, and He will bless you in the land which the Lord your God is giving you." Do you see that? He has COMMANDED you to be BLESSED! Hallelujah that is some Good News!

I love what Boaz says to Ruth in Ruth 2:12, "The Lord repay your work, and a full reward be given you by the Lord God of Israel, *under whose wings you have come for refuge*." (Emphasis Added). We find Ruth making a similar statement when she approaches Boaz to ask him for his mercy on her as her kinsman redeemer in Ruth 3:9-10 (AMP). "⁹ And he said, Who are you? And she answered, I am Ruth your maidservant. *Spread your wing [of protection] over your maidservant, for you are a next of kin.* ¹⁰ And he said, Blessed be you of the Lord, my daughter." (Emphasis Added). Did you also see Boaz's reply? "Be Blessed daughter." He was pronouncing the Blessing over Ruth just like God has pronounced His Blessing over you and me. The difference is that Boaz was Blessing Ruth for her loyalty to Naomi. God has pronounced the Blessing over us because of Jesus' finished work on the cross. He has Blessed us because of our relationship with Him. The Blessing is the free gift that we receive when we make Jesus Lord of our lives and obey His Word.

Why is any of this important to us? It is important because it not only illustrates Boaz's character, but it also illustrates Jesus' character to us. Boaz is a type of Jesus or a foreshadowing of Jesus, if you will. When Boaz took Ruth to be his wife, he not only saved Ruth, but he also saved her mother-in-law, Naomi. According to the Bible, we are the Bride of Christ, and Jesus in His love has rescued us from our certain poverty and ultimate destruction, brought about by sin (See Revelation 19:7-9, Revelation 21:2, 9). Boaz redeemed and rescued Ruth from her struggle of being a foreigner in a strange land, from trying to make it in life without any support or hope. Boaz gave Ruth access to all that he owned the moment he took her as his bride. Jesus has done the same for us by redeeming us from sin, sickness, and the Curse (See Galatians 3:13-14, 1 Peter 2:24, 2 Corinthians 8:9).

We don't have the time to go into it here, but in Ruth 2:14 there is also a type of communion that Boaz offered to Ruth—wine and bread. A symbol of Jesus' shed blood and broken body, which was sacrificed to restore our relationship with the Father and to make available to us all of the benefits of salvation—healing, wholeness, prosperity, freedom from fear, etc.

Finally, look with me at Malachi 4:2-3, "[2] The Sun of Righteousness [Jesus] will rise **with healing in his wings** for you people who fear my name. You will go out and leap like calves let out of a stall. [3] You will trample on wicked people, because on the day I act they will be ashes under the soles of your feet, says the Lord of Armies." Here again, we see a reference being made to the covering of wings, just as we did in Ruth 2:12 and Ruth 3:9. The wings in all of these instances are a reference to the "wings" of the prayer shawl [the tallit in Hebrew]. When Ruth asked Boaz to cover her with the corner of his garment, she was referring to the corners of his prayer shawl—a symbolic covering as redeemer and husband.

In Mark 5 we read about the woman with the issue of blood who said, "[28] If only I may touch His clothes [the wings of His garment, the tzitzit, or the blue cords which hung from Jesus' prayer shawl], I shall be made well." [29] Immediately the fountain of her blood was dried up, and she felt in her body that she was healed of the affliction. [30] And Jesus, immediately knowing in Himself that power had gone out of Him, turned around in the crowd and said, "Who touched My clothes?" This woman was aware of God's promise in Malachi 4, about healing available to her in the "wings" of Jesus' prayer shawl. She knew that if she could just come under Jesus' wings, that she would be made WHOLE!

Moreover, Psalm 91:1-4 tells us, "He who dwells in the secret place of the Most High shall abide under the shadow of the Almighty. [2] I will say of the Lord, "He is my refuge and my fortress; My God, in Him I will trust." [3] Surely He shall deliver you from the snare of the fowler and from the perilous pestilence. *[4] He shall cover you with His feathers, and under His wings you shall take refuge*; His truth shall be your shield and buckler." (Emphasis Added). God has a covering just for you and me. A covering that will keep us protected and delivered from EVERY ATTACK of the enemy. His covering is the Blessing which is meant to keep us whole and delivered from lack of every kind! Hallelujah!

I want you to know that healing belongs to you just as much as salvation, prosperity, safety, security, peace, and every other facet of THE BLESSING belongs to you. It is yours legally, because Jesus has given it to you. There is absolutely nothing you can do to earn it. It is only received by GRACE through FAITH in Jesus as Lord and SAVIOR (See Ephesians 2:8). God has provided everything you could possibly need and desire and made it available to you through your faith in Jesus. He has made it available to you in abundance and free for the taking—if you will only ask and believe Him for it!

Just like Boaz, who instructed his young men to leave handfuls on purpose for Ruth to gather for herself and for Naomi, God has provided Handfuls on purpose for you! He not only has handfuls, but He has an unlimited storehouse filled with whatever it is that you both need and desire (See Psalm 37:4 and Philippians 4:19).

Nothing is too big or too hard for God! He has your healing, your prosperity, your peace, and your security. He has your protection, your great marriage, great relationships with your kids, great jobs, great friends, and anything else that you can think or imagine (See Ephesians 3:20). The only requirement is that you receive Him as YOUR Kinsman Redeemer—Your Savior. Then receive all that He has for you by faith and through your obedience to His Word. Handfuls on purpose are awaiting you. Believe Him and then receive all that you desire in Jesus Name! God is Good...All The Time! Amen.

Daily Declaration

I declare that God has Blessed me and made everything that I need and desire available to me in Jesus. Because I have received Jesus as my Lord and Savior, the windows of Heaven are opened to me, and God is pouring out His Blessing on my life, my family, my job, my finances, and my relationships. I am so Blessed that I cannot contain it all, and I will live my life being a Blessing to others. I am grateful that lack is not a part of my life. Jesus has made me whole in every area of my life: spirit, soul, body, in my finances, in my health, and in my relationships. There is nothing that I lack because God has made all of His grace abound toward me so that I have ALL sufficiency in ALL things. Thank You Jesus for loving me and for giving me handfuls on purpose. I thank you and receive all that you have for me today, in Jesus' name. Amen.

Day 2

Your Part In The Faith Equation

"Then He touched their eyes, saying, "According to your faith let it
BE to you."

Mark 9:29 (NKJV)

Did you know that most people believe that all that they have
to do is to pray for something and then sit back and wait
patiently for God to move on their behalf? I have often
heard statements from Christians like, "Well, God is in control, maybe
He will answer my prayer and maybe he won't…God is Sovereign
after all, and what He wills, He does."

That line of thinking is only partially correct. God is Sovereign (He
is Supreme, absolute, independent, and self-governing), and He will
answer your prayers. But in order for you to receive answers to your
prayers, you must believe that it is His will to answer your prayers,
and that ***you have*** the petitions you have asked of Him THE
INSTANT THAT YOU PRAY for His intervention and help (See 1
John 5:14-15 and Mark 11:23-24). Your part in the faith equation is
ABSOLUTE CONFIDENCE IN GOD AND HIS WORD.

I cringe when I hear people talk about the sovereignty of God, because most of the time, these people have no idea what the word
sovereignty actually means. In fact, in most cases people only use the

word to sound more intelligent in front of their "church friends," or to explain away their experiences for not receiving what they have prayed for. They say something like, "Well God's sovereign, it must have been His will for us to lose our home, but all things work together for good to those who love God." That is such religious garbage! It is an abuse or twisting of Scripture!

Romans 8:25-30 says, "*25 But if we hope for what we do not see, we eagerly wait for it with perseverance.* 26 Likewise the Spirit also helps in our weaknesses. For we do not know what we should pray for as we ought, but the Spirit Himself makes intercession for us with groanings which cannot be uttered. 27 *Now He who searches the hearts knows what the mind of the Spirit is, because He makes intercession for the saints according to the will of God.* 28 And we know that all things work together for good to those who love God, to those who are the called according to His purpose. 29 For whom He foreknew, He also predestined to be conformed to the image of His Son, that He might be the firstborn among many brethren. 30 *Moreover whom He predestined, these He also called; whom He called, these He also justified; and whom He justified, these He also glorified.*

There are three things I want to point out from this passage:

1. We are to persevere in faith while we are waiting for our prayers to manifest in this natural realm. The word persevere means to: keep at it, to endure, to stick with it, and to insist. Perseverance is remaining constant even when we don't see it working. Faith believes God's Word and obeys Him regardless of what things look like (See 2 Corinthians 5:7).

2. The Holy Spirit intercedes (He pleads, He negotiates, and He intervenes) on our behalf in line with both the Word and the Will of God (which are one in the same thing). God has already illustrated His will for every Born Again Believer in His

Word—The Bible. His will is Wholeness in EVERY area of our lives. If you are lacking in any area, it is clearly not the will of God, but an attack of the enemy.

3. God ONLY receives GLORY when you and I are living BLESSED! He receives glory when we look and live the way He has declared us to be and to live. He is glorified when we represent Him well, living above the effects of the Curse. Our Heavenly Father has given to us everything we could ever need and desire IN CHRIST. He has predestined us for a life filled with VICTORY, LOVE, and THE BLESSING. He has both called and equipped us to live above the curse. He has redeemed us and justified us through Jesus, so that we can stand before Him unashamed and free from guilt. And He has clothed us in His own glory, by creating us in His image and likeness! I love how Pastor Mark Hankins says it, "You look better IN CHRIST than you do outside of Him!"

The next time you hear someone bad-mouthing your Heavenly Father, based on their personal negative experience, I would encourage you to ask them for Scriptural PROOF to back up what they are claiming. Tell them that you need proof from the Word of God to substantiate their accusations. 2 Corinthians 13:1 instructs, "By the mouth of two or three witnesses every word shall be established." The Word of God must be THE FINAL AUTHORITY for our lives. Our experiences or the personal experience of others doesn't change or nullify the truth of the Bible. Just because what we experience is not what the Bible says, that doesn't make God a liar. If there is a disconnect between what the Bible declares and what we are experiencing, we must look at our lives and find out where we are missing it. Once we change our negative words, negative behavior, or negative attitudes, we'll begin experiencing the Blessing of God in our lives. God's

Word works every time. Ask Him to show you where you have gone off course and then ask for His help in getting you where you need to be—He'll do it because He loves you! (For more Scriptural evidence regarding judging a thing based on two or three witnesses also see Deut. 17:6; Deut. 19:15; Matt. 18:16; 1 Tim. 5:19; Hebrews 10:28).

Look what the Bible has to say about people who received answers from God. See if you can find a common theme?

Matthew 8:5-10, 13 states, "[5] Now when Jesus had entered Capernaum, a centurion came to Him, pleading with Him, [6] saying, "Lord, my servant is lying at home paralyzed, dreadfully tormented." [7] And Jesus said to him, "I will come and heal him." [8] The centurion answered and said, "Lord, I am not worthy that You should come under my roof. *But only speak a word, and my servant will be healed.* [9] For I also am a man under authority, having soldiers under me. And I say to this one, 'Go,' and he goes; and to another, 'Come,' and he comes; and to my servant, 'Do this,' and he does it." [10] When Jesus heard it, He marveled, and said to those who followed, "Assuredly, I say to you, I have not found such great faith, not even in Israel! …Then Jesus said to the centurion, *"Go your way; and as you have believed, so let it be done for you." And his servant was healed that same hour.*"

In Mark 5:25-29, 34; we find a similar situation, "[25] Now a certain woman had a flow of blood for twelve years, [26] and had suffered many things from many physicians. She had spent all that she had and was no better, but rather grew worse. [27] When she heard about Jesus, she came behind Him in the crowd and touched His garment. [28] *For she said, "If only I may touch His clothes, I shall be made well."* [29] Immediately the fountain of her blood was dried up, and she felt in her body that she was healed of the affliction…*And He said to her,*

"Daughter, your faith has made you well. Go in peace, and be healed of your affliction."

In Mark 10:46-52 we read about a man named Bartimaeus, "[46] Now they came to Jericho. As He went out of Jericho with His disciples and a great multitude, blind Bartimaeus, the son of Timaeus, sat by the road begging. *[47] And when he heard that it was Jesus of Nazareth, he began to cry out and say, "Jesus, Son of David, have mercy on me!"* [48] Then many warned him to be quiet; but he cried out all the more, "Son of David, have mercy on me!" [49] So Jesus stood still and commanded him to be called. Then they called the blind man, saying to him, "Be of good cheer. Rise, He is calling you." [50] *And throwing aside his garment, he rose and came to Jesus. [51] So Jesus answered and said to him, "What do you want Me to do for you?" The blind man said to Him, "Rabboni, that I may receive my sight." [52] Then Jesus said to him, "Go your way; your faith has made you well." And immediately he received his sight and followed Jesus on the road.*

In every one of these instances, the individual who approached Jesus wanted to receive something which was considered by most to be an impossibility. They came to Him in faith and either asked or acted upon their confidence believing that it was Jesus' WILL for them to HAVE what they desired.

The difference between these people and most of the people who do not receive answers to their prayers, is that those who don't get their answers, don't know the will of God, because they don't know what the Bible has to say about their circumstance. Another reason they don't get what they pray for is because they don't respond in faith believing to receive what they have prayed for and then persevere until it manifests in the natural.

I would encourage you to find out what the Bible has to say before you go to the Lord in prayer. We must learn to fight the good fight of faith like an attorney would fight a case. We need to research the evidence (the precious promises of God found in our Bibles), then we must present that evidence to God, expecting to have Him deliver the verdict concerning our case, in our favor. But we must also understand that the Accuser of the brethren (the Devil, See Revelation 12:10), will fight us the whole way, trying to get us to doubt God's love for us, His will for our lives, and His ability to come through for us. The Good News is however, if you persevere in faith you are guaranteed to prevail over all the attacks of the enemy! If God is for us, then who can stand against us! I pray that you understand that we have a responsibility when it comes to prayer. We have the responsibility to make Jesus Lord of our lives first and foremost, we have the responsibility to learn God's Word and promises so that we know what belongs to us as joint-heirs with Christ, and we have the responsibility to believe and to persevere in faith until we receive His promise. Just as Jesus declared to those who wanted to be healed, whole, and lacking nothing, I am declaring to you today, *"**According to your faith** let it **BE** unto you!"*

Daily Declaration

I declare that I am part of the Body of Christ. I declare that God is for me and has planned for me to succeed in life. I declare that I am who God says I am, that I have what He said I have, and that I can do all that He said I can do. I refuse every bit of the curse. Devil, I rebuke you in the name of Jesus and command you to flee from me, my family, my possessions, and all of my circumstances. You have no part in my life! I am a child of the Most High God and Jesus is the Lord of my life. I Am Blessed coming in and going out. I am Blessed in my storehouses (my checking and savings accounts)! My children are Blessed! My home is Blessed! My Career is Blessed! My Health is Blessed! My Mind is Blessed! And everything that I put my hand to prospers in the name of Jesus! I declare that I have the uncommon favor of God operating in every facet of my life and that I have and will overcome every obstacle that the enemy will try to bring against me in Jesus' name! I Thank you Lord Jesus, for fighting my battles and for bringing me victory in every one of them. I love You, and thank You for being my Lord and Savior Jesus! I ask you to lead and to direct my every step today and to be a Blessing to all of the people that I interact with today, in Jesus' mighty name. Amen.

Day 3

Adversity Always Precedes Advancement

"Then the Lord said to Moses, [2] "Tell the Israelites to turn back and encamp near Pi Hahiroth, between Migdol and the sea. They are to encamp by the sea, directly opposite Baal Zephon. [3] Pharaoh will think, 'The Israelites are wandering around the land in confusion, hemmed in by the desert.' [4] And I will harden Pharaoh's heart, and he will pursue them. But I will gain glory for myself through Pharaoh and all his army, and the Egyptians will know that I am the Lord." So the Israelites did this…[10] As Pharaoh approached, the Israelites looked up, and there were the Egyptians, marching after them. They were terrified and cried out to the Lord. [11] They said to Moses, "Was it because there were no graves in Egypt that you brought us to the desert to die? What have you done to us by bringing us out of Egypt? [12] Didn't we say to you in Egypt, 'Leave us alone; let us serve the Egyptians'? It would have been better for us to serve the Egyptians than to die in the desert!" [13] Moses answered the people, "Do not be afraid. Stand firm and you will see the deliverance the Lord will bring you today. The Egyptians you see today you will never see again. [14] The Lord will fight for you; you need only to be still."

Exodus 14:1-4, 10-14 (NIV)

O ur God is a God of deliverance. He always provides a Deliverer for His people. He has promised to both care for His people and make a way of escape when they are in trouble, but He always does so in a way that brings Him glory. His provision always illustrates to others that He is God and that He is good to His people. That is one of the reasons why there is always a period of stretching and even adversity, before we move from one level of faith to the next. God wants us to know that He is there for us and He wants others to understand that He will never leave us or forsake us. God isn't putting us through the fire in order to hurt us—He will never do anything to cause harm in the process of promoting us. Yet we sometimes experience seasons that are filled with trials, tribulations, and difficult obstacles because we live in a fallen world. And when these trials occur in our lives, we question whether or not we have missed God or we question why He has allowed them to occur in the first place. That is all part of being human.

I believe that if I asked each of you if you were exactly where you thought you would be by this time in your life; 95% if not 100% would tell me that you aren't. How many of you have experienced a trial in your health during this last year? How many of you have had a financial setback which has caused you to question some things you were certain God had instructed you to do? How many of you would say that you feel like Breakthrough has continued to elude you for one reason or another? What about your career—How many of you have had difficulties at work or with a boss or a client in the last year? What about a family member? Whatever struggles you have faced this past year, or several years, I don't want us to focus on the problem, but to get our sights set on coming out and overcoming, all the way into our Promised Land.

In Exodus chapter 14, we learn that the Hebrews had once flourished in Egypt and experienced great wealth and freedom there. Yet they had moved from a position of favor with the Egyptians into a life of bondage and being despised. Throughout all of their heartache and hardship, God provided a deliverer—Moses, to bring them out of that adversity and into a place of promotion. When Pharaoh finally allowed the Hebrews to leave Egypt, the Egyptians sent them away loaded with Gold and silver. But once they realized they had just freed their workforce, they reneged and went after them. The attitudes of the Hebrews changed from being joyful and filled with great boldness to fear and horror, thinking that they were going to be slaughtered.

In verses 10-12 (NIV) we read, "[10] As Pharaoh approached, the Israelites looked up, and there were the Egyptians, marching after them. They were terrified and cried out to the Lord. [11] They said to Moses, "Was it because there were no graves in Egypt that you brought us to the desert to die? What have you done to us by bringing us out of Egypt? [12] Didn't we say to you in Egypt, 'Leave us alone; let us serve the Egyptians?" I think that each of us have experienced similar fears and frustrations when we have stepped out to follow the plan of God, that we are certain He has called us to walk out. At first we are exhilarated thinking, "Alright, I'm finally on my way." But when adversity and setbacks come against us, our first thought is often, "Oh no, did I miss God, was it really just me?" We all experience times when the devil tries to get us to question our calling, our mission, and God's plan for our lives.

But look what Moses said to the people when they began questioning their circumstances. "[13] Moses answered the people, "Do not be afraid. Stand firm and you will see the deliverance the Lord will bring you today. The Egyptians you see today you will never see again. [14] The Lord will fight for you; you need only to be still."

Do you understand what it says in verse 13? You may be experiencing adversity in one form or another, but I want to encourage you to remain standing firm in your faith. Just like God told Moses, I'm telling you, your days of sickness, lack, and defeat, are over! God is bringing you out healed, whole, and delivered! I want you to know that that boss or coworker who has been troubling you is about to be moved out of your way and out of your hair. God is going to promote you above them and remove them out of your way. Whatever you are facing, God is bringing you out and into your place of promotion and into your place of Victory!

In Exodus 14:1-2, God tells Moses to make the people camp at Pi Hahiroth. The background to Pi Hahiroth is shady, but many have said that it means "the mouth of water," or "mouth of the gorges." But the Septuagint [the Bible translated into Greek] and some Bible scholars argue that the entomology of Pi Hahiroth leads them to believe that the meaning of that name is: "the mouth to freedom." That was right where God had the Hebrews camping. Though Pharaoh thought that they were in a place of confusion, God was actually setting them up for their amazing journey into freedom. Even in the midst of their adversity and frustration, even though it looked like they were trapped, and would be easy targets, God still protected them from their enemy. The same is true about you! I don't care what your circumstances look like in the natural. You may be surrounded on all sides with adversity and fear closing in around you—but I want you to know that looks can be deceiving. You are at the mouth to your freedom! Keep standing! Keep believing! And keep moving forward in your faith! God is bringing you out of that stuck place and into your next promotion. You're are leaving all of that adversity behind and moving into your place of advancement and Blessing! Amen!

Daily Declaration

I declare right now that I am moving into my place of advancement, my place of promotion, and my place of Super-abundant Blessing and Favor of God! I declare that no weapon which is formed against me shall prosper, and that every tongue which rises against me in judgment, I will condemn in the name of Jesus. I decree and declare that Jesus has delivered me from the curse of sin, sickness, and death, and that every trap that the enemy has set for me, is broken now. I am an ambassador of my Lord Jesus Christ. I am an overcomer in Him! I am more than a conqueror, which means that I win every battle that I'm in, because God fights them for me. If God is for me then who can dare stand against me? I declare that even though my present circumstances may look bleak, I have supernatural hope and faith rising up inside of me. My situations, my circumstances, my health, and my finances are all turning around right now, as I speak! I declare that the Holy Spirit is with me and He is leading me into supernatural victory, favor, increase, and promotion. I will settle for nothing less than God's best for my life. God has said it, I receive it, and that settles it, in Jesus' mighty name, Amen.

Day 4

INCREASE-It Is Gods Will For You!

"^{12} The Lord has been mindful of us, He will bless us: He will bless the house of Israel, He will bless the house of Aaron [the priesthood], ^{13} He will bless those who reverently and worshipfully fear the Lord, both small and great. ^{14} May the Lord give you increase more and more, you and your children. ^{15} May you be blessed of the Lord, Who made heaven and earth!"

Psalm 115:12-15 (AMP)

Every time I see in Scripture that God is mindful of me, that He thinks about me, it reminds me of the song by Israel Houghton, *"I am a friend of God."* This song is based on James 2:23, which says, "^{23} And the Scripture was fulfilled which says, "Abraham believed God, and it was accounted to him for righteousness." And he was called the friend of God." Our faith in God opens up the door to the BLESSING of God, in our lives. Our faith in Him and what He has promised to us, gives Him legal access to operate on our behalf.

In Psalm 8:3-5, the psalmist writes from the perspective of what angels must think about God's deep love for humanity. "When I consider Your heavens, the work of Your fingers, the moon and the stars, which You have ordained, ⁴ What is man that You are mindful of him, and the son of man that You visit him? ⁵ For You have made him a little lower than the angels, and You have crowned him with glory and honor." This tells us that we have been crowned with glory—Is that amazing or what? God has not only BLESSED each and every one of us who are IN CHRIST, but He has given us authority, and crowned us with His glory.

The word glory comes from the Hebrew word *Kabod* which means to be heavy with riches, reputation, honor, and abundance in all things. Though many might argue, Scripture proves that it is God's will for each of His children to BE BLESSED. And just in case you don't already know this, the BLESSING is void of lack, sickness, fear, and every other negative thing.

Psalm 34:8-10 (AMP) says, "⁸ O taste and see that the Lord [our God] is good! Blessed (happy, fortunate, to be envied) is the man who trusts and takes refuge in Him. ⁹ O fear the Lord, you His saints [revere and worship Him]! *For there is no want to those who truly revere and worship Him with godly fear.* ¹⁰ The young lions lack food and suffer hunger, *but they who seek (inquire of and require) the Lord [by right of their need and on the authority of His Word], none of them shall lack any beneficial thing."*

Did you catch that? Those who SEEK, INQUIRE, and REQUIRE of the Lord, based on their authority and understanding of the things that rightfully belong to them from the Word of God—Shall lack no good and beneficial thing. The only lack that you will have is lack of those things belonging to the Curse. However, if you don't know what the Word of God has made available to you, then your lack of understanding will keep you defeated because of your ignorance. Ignorance can kill you!

You cannot fight the enemy solely based on your hopes and wishes. The way that we defeat the enemy is by knowing, understanding, and operating on the promises found in the Bible. The Bible tells us who we are; it defines for us, our identity in Jesus, and it allows us to rest in those promises. As a result, we can then confidently refuse to settle for anything less than what our Heavenly Father has said to us. We are then positive that what we believe; is the will of God for us. That is the point in which we become dangerous to the devil—that is when we become an unstoppable force of faith and light.

Now look with me at Matthew 6:25-34, "[25] Therefore I say to you, do not worry about your life, what you will eat or what you will drink; nor about your body, what you will put on. Is not life more than food and the body more than clothing? [26] Look at the birds of the air, for they neither sow nor reap nor gather into barns; yet your heavenly Father feeds them. Are you not of more value than they? [27] Which of you by worrying can add one cubit to his stature? [28] "So why do you worry about clothing? Consider the lilies of the field, how they grow: they neither toil nor spin; [29] and yet I say to you that even Solomon in all his glory was not arrayed like one of these. [30] Now if God so clothes the grass of the field, which today is, and tomorrow is thrown into the oven, will He not much more clothe you, O you of little faith? [31] "Therefore do not worry, saying, 'What shall we eat?' or 'What shall we drink?' or 'What shall we wear?' [32] For after all these things the Gentiles seek. For your heavenly Father knows that you need all these things. [33] But seek first the kingdom of God and His righteousness, and all these things shall be added to you. [34] Therefore do not worry about tomorrow…"

Why are we told in this passage not to worry about our needs and desires? Because God knows about those things, and as God, He has covenanted to take care of them *ALL* for us. Moreover, He has promised in Psalm 34 that we will lack NO GOOD THING. The questions then become, "Do we believe Him?" And, "Do we trust Him?" It is our job to seek God and to spend time in His Word. Then ALL of our needs and desires will be provided for us. ***GOD IS INCREASE MINDED***! He is always **looking for ways to add** to the lives of His covenant Children, **not to take away from us**. It is our job to **learn to believe and confidently trust Him** for *ALL* that we need and desire. God is not only our source for salvation, but He is our source for every other thing associated with The Abundant Life. Believe and receive all that He has for you today—He's already promised it to you—so why don't you receive it by faith right now?

Daily Declaration

Heavenly Father, I receive all that you have for me today. I declare that I am rich according to 2 Corinthians 8:9. Jesus became poor that I would be made rich in Him. I declare that there is no lack in my life. I am fully supplied and I lack no good thing, in Jesus' name. I have been Blessed so that I may be a Blessing to others. I declare that I am Healed and whole in every part of my spirit, soul, and body. 1 Peter 2:24 declares that Jesus bore my sins in His body, so that I would BE HEALED. I take my healing and I receive it by faith now. I command my body to line up with the Word of God right NOW! I command that every tissue, every cell, every bone, every atom, and every fiber in my body, to function at perfectly, in the name of Jesus! Heavenly Father, thank you for Your amazing love and favor in my life. I receive *ALL* of the Blessing and Increase that you have planned for me—In Jesus' name, Amen.

Day 5

Becoming And Remaining Victory Minded

"So [Israel] came up to Baal-Perazim, and David smote [the Philistines] there. Then David said, God has broken my enemies by my hand, like the bursting forth of waters. Therefore they called the name of that place Baal-Perazim [Lord of breaking through]."

1 Chronicles 14:11 (AMP)

One of the things that I love most about reading the Bible is that even though the Israelites faced many obstacles getting to where God had called them, even though they faced many challenges overcoming the giants that stood before them, they still found the courage to remain victory minded. They learned to take specific steps in order to remind themselves of all the good things that God had done for them. Though they fumbled with doubt and unbelief just like the rest of us, they usually found ways to encourage themselves when opposition returned. And though they blew it horribly in the desert, they learned to focus on the promises of God instead of focusing on their problems. We need to do the same thing in our lives. We need to build alters of remembrance so that when adversity strikes we can say,

"God brought us through that trial and He gave us the victory, He will certainly do it again."

Of course, there were times when the people would get off track. There were times when they became overwhelmed with bouts of negativity. But without fail, God would find a leader who was committed to Him and who would focus on His promises. He would raise up a leader who would overlook their present circumstances and remember His faithfulness. A man or woman of faith, who would lead His people out of *Lo Debar* (the land of lack and not enough) into the land of More Than Enough.

One of the things that the Hebrews were famous for was building alters or memorials to God, that would remind them of God's faithfulness. As I said earlier these alters were markers that would help them remember that if God honored His Word last time, He would do it again, and get them through their current dilemma. These spiritual markers would remind them that no matter what they were currently facing, no matter who was coming against them, nothing was too big for their God. If their God was for them, then who could dare stand against them? (See Romans 8:31).

In Genesis 22 we find the story of Abraham who had been promised an heir (Isaac). Years went by as He waited for the promise to manifest in the natural. Finally, God made good on His promise. But when Isaac was just a young boy, God told Abraham to sacrifice Isaac as an offering to Him. It had to be the most heart-wrenching experience that Abraham had ever experienced; yet, Abraham knew that God would never make a promise that He would not keep.

Numbers 23:19 says, "God is not a man, that He should lie, nor a son of man, that He should repent. Has He said, and will He not do? Or has He spoken, and will He not make it good?" Abraham's confidence in God and His promises enabled him to remain committed as

God's covenant partner, even during this horrific test. He knew that no matter what happened God would somehow raise Isaac back up from the dead, if need be, in order to fulfill His covenant promise and make Abraham a great nation through Isaac.

As Abraham laid Isaac on the altar and was about to follow through with the sacrifice, an angel stopped him immediately and said, "[12] Lay not thine hand upon the lad, neither do thou anything unto him: for now I know that thou fearest God, seeing thou hast not withheld thy son, thine only son from me. [13] And Abraham lifted up his eyes, and looked, and behold behind him a ram caught in a thicket by his horns: and Abraham went and took the ram, and offered him up for a burnt offering in the stead of his son. [14] And Abraham called the name of that place Jehovah Jireh [Yahweh Yireh - which means the God who sees your need beforehand and therefore provides]: as it is said to this day, in the mount of the Lord it shall be seen." (Genesis 22:12-14, KJV).

Do you see that? Abraham built an altar in that place to re-member God's faithfulness in his life. Every time Abraham or his descendants would pass by that place for centuries forward, they would point to that mountain and say, "That is where God provided for Abraham and Isaac. That is the place that God showed Himself strong and provided a Breakthrough out of thin air." Then they would say to one another, "And because God is no respecter of persons, He will do the same for us, because we are covenant children also." (See Romans 2:11 and Acts 10:34).

In Genesis chapter 21, we read about Abraham and Abimelech becoming covenant partners. Abimelech recognized God's favor and increase on Abraham's life and he wanted to make peace between the two of them. "[22] At that time Abimelech and Phicol the commander of his army said to Abraham, God is with you in everything you do. [23] So now, swear to me here by God that you will not deal falsely with me or with my son or with my posterity; but as I have dealt with you kindly, you will do the same with me and with the land in which you have sojourned. [24] And Abraham said, I will swear. [25] When Abraham complained to and reasoned with Abimelech about a well of water [Abimelech's] servants had violently seized, [26] Abimelech said, I know not who did this thing; you did not tell me, and I did not hear of it until today. [27] So Abraham took sheep and oxen and gave them to Abimelech, and the two men made a league or covenant. [28] Abraham set apart seven ewe lambs of the flock, [29] and Abimelech said to Abraham, What do these seven ewe lambs which you have set apart mean? [30] He said, you are to accept these seven ewe lambs from me as a witness for me that I dug this well. [31] Therefore that place was called Beersheba [well of the oath], because there both parties swore an oath." (Genesis 21:22-31, AMP). Abraham again made a memorial out of that well to signify the importance of that unbreakable covenant between the two men. He built the altar for himself and for his people, to serve as a reminder that there was a covenant between them and Abimelech's people, which could not be broken for any reason.

As we discussed a few days ago, when God was bringing Moses and the Hebrews out of captivity in Egypt, He told them to camp at a place called Pi-Hahiroth. God did this because He wanted to rid His people of their problems once and for all. They had been mistreated; they had faced 400 years of abuse and adversity, and He wanted them to never again fear their enemies. He wanted to take them over into their Promised Land, focused on His goodness, not looking back over their shoulders wondering if they'd be captured and taken back into slavery and abuse.

Even as the Egyptians pursued the Hebrews, it "looked as if" they would be captured or possibly even killed in the desert. They were surrounded on all sides and had nowhere to turn, but to the sea. The sea "looked like" an impassable obstacle for such a multitude of people. The Bible says, "Then the Lord said to Moses, [2] Tell the Israelites to turn back and encamp near Pi Hahiroth, between Migdol and the sea. They are to encamp by the sea, directly opposite Baal Zephon. [3] Pharaoh will think, the Israelites are wandering around the land in confusion, hemmed in by the desert." (See Exodus 14:1-3, NIV). Remember, "it looked as if" they were HEMMED IN, TRAPPED, and FACING CERTAIN AHNIALATION, but once again, God brought them out of their adversity and into victory! He brought them from a place that "looked" inescapable and into a place called Pi-Hahiroth (or the MOUTH OF FREEDOM).

As Moses obeyed the commanded of God to lift his staff and point it over the sea, the water parted and the Hebrews traveled safely through on dry land. But as the Egyptians pursued them, they were swallowed-up and destroyed. Exodus 14:26-31 (NIV) says, "[26] Then the Lord said to Moses, "Stretch out your hand over the sea so that the waters may flow back over the Egyptians and their chariots and horsemen." [27] Moses stretched out his hand over the sea, and at daybreak the sea went back to its place. The Egyptians were fleeing toward it, and the Lord swept them into the sea. [28] The water flowed back and covered the chariots and horsemen—the entire army of Pharaoh that had followed the Israelites into the sea. Not one of them survived. [29] But the Israelites went through the sea on dry ground, with a wall of water on their right and on their left. [30] That day the Lord saved Israel from the hands of the Egyptians, and Israel saw the Egyptians lying dead on the shore. [31] And when the Israelites saw the mighty hand of the Lord displayed against the Egyptians, the people feared the Lord and put their trust in him and in Moses his servant."

In 1 Chronicles 14, we read about the Philistines who have become a problem for David. We then find David praying and asking God to give Him victory over His foes. As a result God says to Him, "Go up, for I will deliver them into your hand." (Verse 10). David Obeys God and we read, "So [Israel] came up to Baal-Perazim, and David smote [the Philistines] there. Then David said, God has broken my enemies by my hand, like the bursting forth of waters. Therefore they called the name of that place Baal-Perazim [Lord of breaking through]." (Verse 11, AMP). In other words, God provided David and His people Israel, a tsunami sized victory. It wasn't just a little win. No! God came in like a flood and overpowered and overwhelmed Israel's enemies. David then built an altar in that place and called it "The God of the Breakthrough."

What memorials do you have in your lives that force you to maintain a victory mindset? What triumphs has God caused you to have that illustrate to you and your family, that no matter what you may be facing, you can rest assured that your covenant keeping God will bring you over into the land of More Than Enough? What altars remind you that God has always been faithful to you and your family? What promises prove to you that He will take you from *Lo Debar* to your Promised Land? What monuments have been set-up or established in your spirit, that remind you that if God is for you then nothing and no one can stand against you? What promises from the Word of God have been written on your heart and have given you the confidence to believe that no weapon formed against you will prosper? What experiences have caused you to know that you know that you know, that no sickness, that no lack, that no set back, no part of the curse has the power to stick to you, because you are an heir of the Kingdom of God?

If you don't have any altars that you have built to remind you of God's constant faithfulness, then start building them from this moment forward. If you do have them, then give God a shout of praise and thank Him for giving you something to shout about! Those who are Victory Minded will always enjoy the best that God has for them! I believe that you are at the right place at the right time to experience more of God's Blessing and to achieve greater things than you could ever dream or imagine—just keep walking in your Victory! You've got the Victory In Jesus now! God ALWAYS causes you to triumph in Him (1 Corinthians 15:57 and 2 Corinthians 2:14).

Daily Declaration

In the name of Jesus, I declare that I am VICTORIOUS in all things In Christ Jesus! I know beyond any shadow of a doubt that God is for me, that I am an overcomer, and that I am Blessed with EVERY spiritual Blessing In Christ. God has said in His Word that He will not only provide all of my needs (Philippians 4:19), but that He will also give me the desires of my heart because I delight myself In Him. Father I thank you for Jesus and I thank you for Your Holy Spirit in operation in my life. I declare from this moment forward that I will build spiritual altars to remind myself and my family of your faithfulness to us. Whenever trouble, adversity, and trials try to come my way and cause me to doubt, I will remember back on all of the good things you have done for me. I will stir-up my faith and continue to believe you for my breakthrough. Father, I declare that Your Word is true. I know that you cannot lie. I know that you love me and want me to be Blessed. And as a result, I declare that I am everything that You have declared me to be in Jesus name. Amen.

Day 6

Don't Allow Satan To Choke The Life Out Of You

"And it came to pass in our going on to prayer, a certain maid, having a spirit of Python, did meet us, who brought much employment to her masters by soothsaying."

Acts 16:16 (Young's Literal Translation)

I would be willing to bet that most of us are familiar with this passage of Scripture, but that most of us have not seen it quite this way before. We've read about the Apostle Paul and Silas who were led by the Holy Spirit to Philippi, but once they showed up there, a woman controlled by demonic spirits troubled them. Acts 16:16-19 (NKJV) reads this way, "16 Now it happened, as we went to prayer, that a certain slave girl *possessed with a spirit of divination* met us, who brought her masters much profit by fortune-telling. 17 This girl followed Paul and us, and cried out, saying, "These men are the servants of the Most High God, who proclaim to us the way of salvation." 18 And this she did for many days. But Paul, greatly annoyed, turned and said to the spirit, "I command you in the name of Jesus Christ to come out of her." And he came out that very hour."

The Orthodox Jewish Bible reads, "A certain *shifchah* [hand-maid, female slave, or a female servant] having a *ruach* [spirit] of the python (i.e., a shed, demon) came out to meet us." The Complete Jewish Bible reads, "…a slave girl who had in her a snake-spirit that enabled her to predict the future."

I find this very interesting. The literal translation from the Greek says that this woman was possessed by a demonic, snake-like spirit, or a python spirit, which choked the life out of her and kept her in bondage. She had become a slave because of all of the money that she could make for her owners through fortune telling. I want to ask you an important question. Are you allowing the devil to keep you prisoner to sin and choke the life out of you, like he was this young slave girl?

Throughout the Bible Satan is called a serpent, a dragon, and the Accuser of the Brethren. In Genesis 3:1-5 we find Satan tempting Eve. The Bible says, "[1]Now *the serpent was more cunning than any beast of the field* which the Lord God had made. *And he said to the woman*, "Has God indeed said, 'You shall not eat of every tree of the garden'?" [2] And the woman said to the serpent, "We may eat the fruit of the trees of the garden; [3] but of the fruit of the tree which is in the midst of the garden, God has said, 'You shall not eat it, nor shall you touch it, lest you die.'" [4] Then the serpent said to the woman, "You will not surely die. [5] For God knows that in the day you eat of it your eyes will be opened, and you will be like God, knowing good and evil.""

In Revelation 12:9-11 we're told, "[9] So *the great dragon* was cast out, *that serpent of old*, *called the Devil and Satan*, who deceives the whole world; he was cast to the earth, and his angels were cast out with him. [10] Then I heard a loud voice saying in heaven, "Now salvation, and strength, and the kingdom of our God, and the power of His

Christ have come, for **the accuser of our brethren**, who accused them before our God day and night, has been cast down. [11] And they overcame him by the blood of the Lamb and by the word of their testimony, and they did not love their lives to the death.

Revelations 20:1-3 tells us, "Then I saw an angel coming down from heaven, having the key to the bottomless pit and a great chain in his hand. [2] *He laid hold of the dragon, that serpent of old, who is the Devil and Satan*, and bound him for a thousand years; [3] and he cast him into the bottomless pit, and shut him up, and set a seal on him, so that he should deceive the nations no more..."

The thing that I want to point out is that we are told that the Devil is crafty, that he is cunning, and that he cannot be trusted (Genesis 3:1). Jesus warned His Disciples when he sent them out in Matthew 10:16, "Behold, I send you out as sheep in the midst of wolves. Therefore be wise [Greek- *phronimos* – wise, intelligent, prudent, mindful of, having a proper perspective of the truth, or to be shrewd] as serpents and harmless as doves."

On January 8, 2004 men in Jakarta, Indonesia caught the largest reticulated python ever, which measured in at 48 feet 8 inches long and weighed 983 pounds. Snakes like these are notorious for squeezing the life out of humans and consuming them whole.

In other words, Jesus was saying to them that they were to be cautious, smart, savvy, and sensible. He was telling them that they needed to understand the truth about the things they would undoubtedly encounter, knowing that the devil roams about like a lion seeking whom he may devour (1 Peter 5:8). Satan knew the truth, but he lied to Eve when he tempted her to disobey God. Just like he lied to Eve, our circumstances will lie to us, that is why we walk by faith and not by sight (2 Corinthians 5:7). If we become controlled by our senses we'll lose every time—instead we must be ruled by the Word of God and led by the Holy Spirit and anointed with His power.

Sin is sneaky and it will always try to creep up on us from out of nowhere. It has a notorious reputation for appearing harmless, but like a python, it will try to squeeze the life out of us. Satan is a liar, he is the Father of Lies (John 8:44) and he can never tell the truth, because there is no truth in him. He will make promises that may sound good, but they will end in death. That is why we need to be as wise as serpents, but as harmless as doves. We are to understand our enemy and his tactics. Even though he may promise the world to us—he can never deliver, and he wouldn't even if he could. His only mission is to deceive, and to steal, to kill, and to destroy—or to try to strangle us in his python grip.

Don't fall for the lies that he will try to feed you. He is like a snake charmer who continually tries to mesmerize us with soft and sweet music, but in reality he's lining up for his deadly strike. Satan has nothing to offer us that is worth our attention. His promises may look appealing at first glance, they may seem enticing, but they always end up choking the life out of all who take him up on his offer. Instead keep your eyes on Jesus, the author and finisher of our faith.

Daily Declaration

I bind you Satan, in the mighty name of Jesus! You have no legal right to operate in my life because I am a child of God. I declare that Jesus is the Lord of my life, and my allegiance is to Him, to my Heavenly Father, to the Holy Spirit, and to my brothers and sisters in Christ only. I declare that I am a doer of the Word and not a hearer only. I hear what my Father says to me and that is what I do. I declare that I am as wise as a serpent and as harmless as a dove. That I am wise to your motives and tactics Satan, but that I reject all of them and continue to walk by faith and to operate in the Agape love of God. In the name of Jesus, I break all of your power, your attacks, and your python grip off of my life, off of the lives of my children, and off of all my circumstances, off of possessions, off of my finances, and off of my career. I render you harmless and ineffective against me devil, in Jesus mighty name. The Bible says in 1 Peter 5:8 that if I humble myself under the mighty hand of God, and if I cast all of my cares onto Him, He will exalt me in due time. I submit myself and all that I have to the authority of my Heavenly Father and to my Savior Jesus! I cast all of my cares and concerns over onto God. The Bible says that when I do this, that I am resisting you and that you must flee from me. Devil, I command that you take your slimy, scaly, snake-like self out of my life, in the name of Jesus! I declare that you are defeated, that God is exalted, and that Jesus is the Lord of my life! I decree that I am Blessed, I am Victorious, and I am Highly Favored by the Most High God—El Shaddai—The God of More Than Enough! I pray all of this in Jesus' name, Amen!

Day 7

Have You Received Your Vaccination?

"²⁰ My son, attend to my words; consent and submit to my sayings.
²¹ Let them not depart from your sight; keep them in the center of your heart. ²² For they are life to those who find them, healing and health to all their flesh."

Proverbs 4:20-22 (AMP)

How many of you have ever received a vaccination? What is a vaccination? According to the Merriam Webster dictionary, a vaccination is: "A preparation of killed microorganisms, living attenuated organisms, or living fully virulent organisms that is administered to produce or artificially increase immunity to a particular disease."

Well guess what? When Jesus was crucified and raised from the dead, sin was conquered for good! Sin's power was defeated or you could say it was crushed—killed—and no longer had authority in the lives of those belonging to God.

1 Corinthians 15:54-58 says, "⁵⁴ So when this corruptible has put on incorruption, and this mortal has put on immortality, then shall

be brought to pass the saying that is written: "Death is swallowed up in victory." [55] "O Death, where is your sting? "O Hades, where is your victory?" [56] The sting of death is sin, and the strength of sin is the law. [57] But thanks be to God, who gives us the victory through our Lord Jesus Christ. [58] Therefore, my beloved brethren, be steadfast, immovable, always abounding in the work of the Lord, knowing that your labor is not in vain in the Lord." WOW! I receive that in the name of Jesus!

You may be asking, "What are these Scriptures talking about?" They are referring to the time when this corruptible [or our fallen human spirit has], put on incorruption [that time when we receive the fulfillment of _**ALL**_ that Jesus has done for us spirit, soul, and body. It is not only referring to that moment when we received Jesus as the Lord of our life. But the time when we recognize that salvation is freedom from every aspect of the curse]. It is referring to life on earth **RIGHT NOW** for Believers and the time when we will experience the fullness of God's promise at the resurrection of the Saints. It is referring to our present understanding that sin and death no longer have power over us. That we have become totally free from the power of sickness, lack, and spiritual death and have gained victory over all of these things through Jesus who is our victory! Amen!

These verses mean more to us however, because they also refer to the soon approaching time when Jesus takes His place as the returning and Triumphant King of kings and Lord of lords. The time when Satan and his demons have been thrown in the pit of Hell; and the resurrection of the dead has been completed. It is referring to the time when there is no more sickness, disease, sorrow, or death in operation. (See Revelation 21:4). What can a dead, illegal, unproductive curse do against the power of the blood of Jesus?

Look at Matthew 16:15-19, "[15] He [Jesus] said to them, "But who do you say that I am?" [16] Simon Peter answered and said, "You are the Christ, the Son of the living God." [17] Jesus answered and said to him, "Blessed are you, Simon Bar-Jonah, for flesh and blood has not revealed this to you, but My Father who is in heaven. [18] And I also say to you that you are Peter, and on this rock I will build My church, and *the gates of Hades shall not prevail against it [you]. [19] And I will give you the keys of the kingdom of heaven, and whatever you bind on earth will be bound in heaven, and whatever you loose on earth will be loosed in heaven*."

What just happened here? Jesus asked the disciples to tell Him who He was. Peter replied, "You are the anointed One, the promised Messiah." And as a result, Jesus praises Peter, stating that Yes, Peter was correct. He also told them that He had received that revelation knowledge from God, and that it was that knowledge which allowed him to understand the truth of Jesus identity. Jesus then tells them that it is upon that revelation knowledge about who He was, that He would build His Church. He wasn't saying He would build His Church on PETER whose Greek name meant rock. No, He was saying that the Church would be built on the revelation or the enlightenment of those who recognized ALL that Jesus IS.

Why would Jesus build His Church on the revelation of His anointing? Look at Isaiah 10:27 (KJV), "And it shall come to pass in that day, that his burden shall be taken away from off thy shoulder, and his yoke from off thy neck, and the yoke shall be destroyed because of the anointing." Jesus is the anointing; He is the Anointed One, The Messiah, who takes away the sin and burden of the world. The Bible says that He came to seek and to save the lost—or those without hope. (See Luke 19:10).

In John 1:29, John the Baptist says, "[29]…Behold! The Lamb of God who takes away the sin of the world!" Let me ask you a couple of questions. Is sickness part of the curse? Is it a result of sin in the earth? It sure is, if you don't believe me read the entire chapter of Deuteronomy 28, which talks about both the Blessing and the Curse.

Now look at Matthew 11:29-30, "Take My yoke upon you and learn from Me, for I am gentle and lowly in heart, and you will find rest for your souls. [30] For My yoke is easy and My burden is light." What does Jesus mean when He says that His yoke is light? He means that when you are tied or connected to Him, there is no connection to the curse. He is saying that the curse cannot stick to Him—He is immune to it! He is saying that sin has no authority in His life and that He forbids it to enter in and stay anywhere He is—He rebukes it—He commands it to FLEE and so should we! If we are where He is—then sin cannot remain there! Hallelujah! I'm sticking with Jesus—how about you?

Now that we know this, let's go back to Proverbs 4:20-22 and decipher what God is saying about His Word. "[20] My son, attend to my words; consent and submit to my sayings. [21] Let them not depart from your sight; keep them in the center of your heart. [22]For they are life to those who find them, healing and health to all their flesh." What does it mean to attend to something or someone? It means to give a great deal of attention to something, to care for it, to esteem it, or to place a high value upon His Word.

God then says, "Submit to my sayings." Submitting to something means that you bow down before it or that you serve it respectfully, as you would someone who is over you. The next thing that God instructs us to do, is to keep His Words before us, to use His Word as the directing light of our vision, to make it the pinnacle guide for our spirit man (and to deposit it into the core of our being). He promises that by doing so, it will bring to us life and healing *in **ALL** of our flesh*.

The interesting thing is that the word healing is derived from the Hebrew word *marpe*, which is the Hebrew word for medicine, remedy, or cure. ***God's Word is THE CURE to all of sin's symptoms***! God is saying that when we submit to His Word and when we keep it as our guiding force, we are in essence inoculated, vaccinated, and immunized, against ALL of sin's devices to steal, kill, and destroy us. Sin no longer has any power in our lives unless we allow it to remain there.

I pray that you begin to fully understand today, ALL that Jesus has done for you on the cross. I pray that you receive the revelation knowledge from your Heavenly Father, which will build inside of you the understanding that you have been vaccinated against every symptom of sin. God has given you the remedy to sin. He has given you the cure and that cure is Jesus! JESUS IS THE LIVING WORD—THE ANOINTED ONE and HIS ANOINTING! Take God's medicine, His remedy, His vaccination today! Take God's Word and begin speaking His promises over your life. Receive by faith the freedom from sin, sickness and the curse—that God has provided for you! Victory, Healing, and Breakthrough, is yours according to the Word of God. Have you received your vaccination?

Daily Declaration

I receive my Word vaccination today in the name of Jesus! I declare that the Word is working mightily in my life, in my finances, in my relationships, in my career, in my children, and in my body. I declare that I have been redeemed from the curse of sin, sickness, and death, according to Galatians 3:13-14 and Deuteronomy 28. I declare that the anointing power of Jesus is alive and working in me, around me, and through me, in the name of Jesus! Father, I thank you today for Your revelation knowledge of who I am in you and who you are in me. I am who you say I am, I receive all that you have for me, and I will do all that you have called me to do. You have a great and wonderful plan and purpose for my life. I declare that I will find it, I will cultivate it, and I will fulfill it, in the name of Jesus, Amen.

Day 8

Have You Forgotten Your Prosperity?

"¹⁷ You have moved my soul far from peace; *I have forgotten prosperity.* ¹⁸ And I said, "My strength and my hope have perished from the Lord."

Lamentations 3:17-18 (NKJV)

I am so thankful that Jesus' sacrifice on the cross gave us all access to the BLESSING. I have heard people make excuses as to why Christians are not supposed to be prosperous. Some have even rationalized why prosperity is a "bad thing." Many have made it their life's mission to educate everyone else about their personal opinion. I have heard numerous debates surrounding this subject, and have witnessed name calling and outright division within the body of Christ. All of this strife is alive in the Church, simply because of false information these people have received, because of their pride, because of the deception of the enemy, and because of a lack of understand regarding what Scripture teaches about prosperity.

If prosperity is so bad, then why is everyone trying to become something that they perceive as being evil? What is the point of working hard and going your business? Why invest and save for the future? Why dream about vacations, leisure with family, and that wonderful retirement? If prosperity is so evil then having thoughts of a bright future are evil. Let me ask you another question. Why do people flock to the United States of America, in search of a better life and unlimited opportunity? The truth is—instinctively, we all know that prosperity is good! Prosperity allows us to be a Blessing to others. Prosperity is part of the Blessing of God and one aspect of the benefits that are made available to us as joint-heirs with Christ.

When we talk about prosperity—we are not just referring to money or material increase. Prosperity includes so much more. True prosperity, God's definition of prosperity, includes spiritual Increase, mental and emotional soundness, physical wholeness, and relational well-being and multiplication. At the same time the Bible is replete with references to financial and material prosperity, so we must not exclude it from our understanding of Biblical prosperity.

Proverbs 10:22 declares, "The blessing of the Lord makes one rich, and He adds no sorrow with it." 3 John 2 states, "Beloved, I pray that you may prosper in all things and be in health, just as your soul prospers." Psalm 35:27 tells us, "Let them shout for joy and be glad, who favor My righteous cause; and let them say continually, "Let the Lord be magnified, Who has pleasure in the prosperity of His servant." And what about Psalm 115:12-14 which says, "[12] The Lord has been mindful of us; He will bless us; He will bless the house of Israel; He will bless the house of Aaron. [13] He will bless those who fear the Lord, both small and great.[14] May the Lord give you increase more and more, you and your children."

Since we are sure that prosperity, increase, and wholeness are all part of God's will for His Children, then the question becomes, "Why aren't more Christians living the Abundant Life He has promised in the Bible?" Or stated another way, "If it is God's will for His people to be Blessed, then why do so many of them look cursed?"

Proverbs 26:1-2 (NLT) gives us a hint, "[1]Honor is no more associated with fools than snow with summer or rain with harvest. [2] Like a fluttering sparrow or a darting swallow, *an undeserved curse will not land on its intended victim*." The King James says it this way, "*…the curse causeless shall not come.*" What does that mean? It means that **THERE IS A REASON** for disaster, **THERE IS A REASON** that the curse is operating in a person's life. The answer is: a door has been opened to the enemy, who is always seeking for ways to bring destruction and defeat through stealing, killing, and destroying. (See Genesis 4:7; John 10:10; 1 Peter 5:8).

Just as the curse can only come to a person as a result of opening a door to Satan, the BLESSING comes by opening up ourselves to God. It comes to us when we open up the door of our heart to Jesus and invite Him in to become Lord of our life. Once we take that first crucial step, Jesus brings with Him His Holy Spirit, to lead, to guide, and to deliver us from every aspect of the Curse. He gives back to us everything that the Devil stole when he deceived Adam and Eve in the Garden. Jesus regained possession of all those things when He made a show of Satan in Hell. Jesus defeated Satan and stripped him of all authority, when He made His sacrificial offering for us through His death, burial, and resurrection.

In Colossians 2:10-15 (NKJV) we read about ourselves, "**[10] and you are complete** [you lack nothing] *in Him* [Jesus], who is the head of all principality and power. [11] In Him you were also circumcised with the circumcision made without hands, by putting off the body of the

47

sins of the flesh, by the circumcision of Christ, [12] buried with Him in baptism, in which you also were raised with Him through faith in the working of God, who raised Him from the dead. [13] And you, being dead in your trespasses and the uncircumcision of your flesh, He has made alive together with Him, having forgiven you all trespasses, [14] having wiped out the handwriting of requirements that was against us, which was contrary to us. And He has taken it out of the way, having nailed it to the cross. [15] *Having disarmed principalities and powers, He made a [show – KJV] public spectacle of them, triumphing over them in it."* (Emphasis Added).

The entire Bible is a testimony to the truth that Satan is a defeated foe. It is a treatise to the fact that we truly are more than conquerors IN CHRIST. The sad thing is: too many Christians are living below their rightful position as joint heirs with Christ (See Romans 8:17). Many have been deceived into believing that prosperity only alludes to money—and that money is bad and dirty thing. Some have even been connived and hoodwinked into assuming that if a person was truly holy, he or she would be willing to give up everything they have, and live in abject poverty. Both of these ideas are wrong. True Biblical prosperity is wholeness in man's spirit, soul, body, relationships, and material goods. I want you to know that money isn't evil; it is simply a tool that we use in the worlds system to purchase the things that we need and desire. The only thing concerning money that has the ability to be evil is our attitudes about it. It is only when we put our desire for money above our desire for God and His principles—that those pursuits become evil. Money itself is neutral.

1 Timothy 6:9-10 (NKJV) explains it this way, "[9] But those who desire to be rich fall into temptation and a snare, and into many foolish and harmful lusts which drown men in destruction and perdition. [10] **For <u>the love of money</u> is a root of all kinds of evil, for which**

some have strayed from the faith in their greediness, and pierced themselves through with many sorrows."

It is the desire for riches and what they offer, over the desire for God and what He has already done for us; that is evil. It is the act of worshiping money and what it can buy, instead of worshiping God who is the creator of all things and who gives all things to us richly to enjoy—that is evil. (See 1 Timothy 6:17). In reality, all evil is based on one thing—Selfishness. When we become selfish and put those selfish desires over God and over others, then evil rules our lives. God is Love and He has poured out an overflowing abundance of love in our hearts. When we stop operating in love and begin operating from the standpoint of selfish desires—then we shut everything and every-one else out of our lives. We forget about the Creator and begin to focus solely on what we can take from Him and others instead of how we can Bless Him and others through our acts of love.

1 Corinthians 13:8 tells us that, "Love never fails." We give evil free reign in our lives when we forget where ALL BLESSINGS originate—from God. We then make matters worse by turning away from our faith and from God as our source, and begin trusting in money as our source.

We read it earlier but it bears repeating. The Apostle John illus-trated in 3 John 2 the correct perspective for prosperity when he said, "[2] Beloved, I pray that you may prosper in all things and be in health, just as your soul prospers." All true prosperity must begin with spiritu-al prosperity which is only found in a relationship with Father, Son, and Holy Spirit. Once our spirit has become prosperous in Jesus, John said that it was God's will for us to prosper in ALL things, including our health and soul.

Now that we have this basic foundation regarding prosperity, let's go back to Lamentations 3:17-18, to discover what is truly being said. "[17] You have moved my soul far from peace; *I have forgotten prosperity.* [18] And I said, "My strength and my hope have perished from the Lord." Just like Job, in Job 3:25, an erroneous statement is being made about God. The writer of Lamentations is blaming God for His cursed state of being, but then he admits that it was he, who forgot about where and what true prosperity entailed. In other words, he gave up on the idea or belief that prosperity belonged to him as a result of covenant relationship with God. Because of his lack of understand about prosperity, he was stuck living a life of anguish, poverty, suffering, all of which are part of the curse. Moreover, he said that his strength [his power] and his hope [his confident understanding of God's will which energizes faith] had perished. In other words, through his ignorance of the truth, he called destruction upon himself.

How did he do this? Wrong thinking always leads to wrong speaking which always leads to wrong results. Proverbs 23:7 tells us that as a man thinks in his heart so is he. Proverbs 18:20-21 then explains that, "[20] A man's stomach shall be satisfied from the fruit of his mouth; from the produce of his lips he shall be filled. [21] Death and life are in the power of the tongue, and those who love it will eat its fruit."

Whatever we believe to be true we will eventually say. It is that simple. It doesn't even matter if those thoughts are actually valid or not. And what we speak, positive or negative, we allow into our lives.

Matthew 18:18-20 (AMP) explains, "[18] Truly I tell you, whatever you forbid and declare to be improper and unlawful on earth must be what is already forbidden in heaven, and whatever you permit and declare proper and lawful on earth must be what is already permitted in heaven. [19] Again I tell you, if two of you on earth agree (harmonize together, make a symphony together) about whatever [anything and everything] they may ask, it will come to pass and be done for them by My Father in heaven. [20] For wherever two or three are gathered (drawn together as My followers) in (into) My name, there I Am in the midst of them."

God is a gentleman; He will not force you to live in the BLESSING if you don't want to. You have a free will to choose how your life will turn out (See Deuteronomy 30:14-20). In fact if you don't believe that prosperity belongs to you IN CHRIST, you have nothing to worry about, you will never experience it! Why? Because everything God does, is a direct result of faith. God is not moved by our needs, He is not moved by lack, He is moved by our faith in Him, and without faith it is **IMPOSSIBLE** to please God. That said; I want you to know that He does care about each and every one of our needs. The problem is that if our needs were what moved God, then all that Satan would need to do to control God would be to create more needs in our life through his stealing, killing, and destroying. But God is the sovereign, not the Devil.

No matter what kind of needs you have, the need for a Savior, the need for healing in your body, or healing in your marriage, the need for soundness in your mind, or great relationships with your kids, or even financial or other material needs or desires, God is willing to provide you with the answer for **ALL** of them! God is not limited in any way and His desire is to give you ALL that He has—after all, He gave His BEST—JESUS. If God is willing to give us Jesus, what is there that He won't give to us? ABSOLUTELY NOTHING!

Don't limit God's ability in your life by forgetting Him or forgetting prosperity. Put everything in the proper order beginning with your love and gratitude for Him, and everything else will fall into place as it should. Seek His Kingdom and His righteousness first, and ALL of the other things you want and need will be provided for you. (Matthew 6:33). Remember what we learned from Psalm 35:27, "Let the Lord be magnified, Who has pleasure in the prosperity of His servant." Learn to magnify God, seek Him and be thankful for all that He is in your life and He will take pleasure in prospering you beyond your wildest dreams and imaginations! God is Good and His will is that you prosper even as your spirit and your soul prosper in Him! Amen!

Daily Declaration

I declare that I have everything that God has made available to me, in Jesus. I am Blessed! I am Prosperous! And I am living the Abundant Life that Jesus came to earth to make available to me! I declare that my health is increasing and that my children are Blessed, saved, and seeking the Lord. I declare that I am prospering in my spirit and in my relationship with my Heavenly Father, His Son Jesus, and the Holy Spirit. I decree that my mind is alert and that my heart is receptive to all that God has to say to me and that I obey His Word. Finally, I declare that I am Blessed coming in and going out, that I am the head and not the tail, that I am above only and not beneath. I command my finances and my bank accounts to BE BLESSED in Jesus' name, Amen.

Day 9

You Were Created To Weather The Storms Of Life Not To Break Under The Pressure

"The [uncompromisingly] righteous shall flourish like the palm tree [be long-lived, stately, upright, useful, and fruitful]; they shall grow like a cedar in Lebanon [majestic, stable, durable, and incorruptible]."

Psalm 92:12 (AMP)

One of the most fascinating facts about palm trees is that they weather storms when everything else around them is destroyed and laid desolate. Even in the most severe hurricanes: Category 5 hurricanes, where the winds are in excess of 155 miles per hour, these amazing trees bend and sway under the pressure, but they are rarely uprooted or broken in two. I've often wondered how they can survive such fierce conditions. As a result of personal study, I've uncovered interesting information about palm trees. If we apply this information to our lives, I believe it will help us weather our storms more successfully and enable us to emerge from them VICTORIOUSLY.

One reason palm trees endure so well under the enormous pressures applied to them during hurricanes, is because they have adapted to compensate for their environment. When the wind begins to pick up they release their palm fronds, so that the winds have less opportunity to grab ahold of them and pull them down. You may think that letting go is a negative attribute, but it is actually a positive one. When the wind begins to whip around these trees, applying pressure to them, they have learned an amazing defense mechanism which helps them to remain standing—they just let go of all of their "baggage,"

This technique reminds me of 1Peter 5:6-7 (NLT) which says, "⁶ So humble yourselves under the mighty power of God, and at the right time He will lift you up in honor. ⁷ *Give all your worries and cares to God, for He cares about you*." (Emphasis Added). In other words, instead of trying to battle against the cyclone winds all by itself, the palm tree has learned to cast its cares, and to release all of the responsibilities for its life, over into the hands of God.

Just like the palm tree has learned to adapt and to withstand the pressures of tsunamis, tempests, and typhoons, we need to come to an understanding that storms will occasionally occur in our own lives. We have an enemy—Satan, whose mission is to steal, to kill, and to destroy. But when the gale force winds of destruction begin to blow our way, it is our job to let go and to let God. We do this, understanding that He won't allow us to be blown over or taken out by the hurricanes of life.

1 Corinthians 10:13 (AMP) describes these types of trials and explains God's sustaining grace when they come our way. "¹³ For no temptation (no trial regarded as enticing to sin), [no matter how it

comes or where it leads] has overtaken you and laid hold on you that is not common to man [that is, no temptation or trial has come to you that is beyond human resistance and that is not adjusted and adapted and belonging to human experience, and such as man can bear]. But God is faithful [to His Word and to His compassionate nature], and He [can be trusted] not to let you be tempted and tried and assayed beyond your ability and strength of resistance and power to endure, but with the temptation He will [always] also provide the way out (the means of escape to a landing place), that you may be capable and strong and powerful to bear up under it patiently."

While most other trees and shrubs would break under such pressure, the palm tree has adapted and has learned to become flexible and to gently bend without snapping. As the torrential rains and winds beat against the palm, it may bend so much that it completely touches the ground. During those times it may look defeated, but when the pressure lets up; it majestically straightens itself, and then stands strong, tall, and victorious in all of its glory.

Micah 7:8 says, "Do not rejoice over me, my enemy; when I fall, I will arise; when I sit in darkness, the Lord will be a light to me." Psalm 37:24 tells us, "Though he fall, he shall not be utterly cast down; for the Lord upholds him with His hand." And Proverbs 24:16 declares, "For a righteous man may fall seven times and rise again, but the wicked shall fall by calamity."

Every time the enemy mounts an attack against us, we've got to understand that God has promised to keep us safely protected and out of harm's reach. Our circumstances may look hopeless, but God has promised us, "[7] A thousand may fall at your side, and ten thousand at your right hand; but it [destruction, harm, and defeat] shall not come near you. [8] Only with your eyes shall you look, and see the reward of the wicked. [9] Because you have made the Lord, who is my refuge, even the Most High, your dwelling place, [10] No evil shall befall you, nor shall any plague come near your dwelling; [11] For He shall give His angels charge over you, to keep you in all your ways." (Psalm 91:7-11).

Another interesting fact about palm trees is that they always weather storms better when they are grouped together as opposed to being alone. The same is true with the people of God. When we receive support, encouragement, and when we can lean on one another, it enables us to get through our own storms better off. That is why belonging to a Church family is so important. We all need people to speak faith and encouragement into us. We all need to be needed by others and to be reassured that we really matter. It is also important that we use our gifts and our callings to help propel the next generation of Believers to grow spiritually and to advance further than ourselves. That is why God's Word says, "We should not stop gathering together with other believers, as some of you are doing. Instead, we must continue to encourage each other even more as we see the day of the Lord coming." (See Hebrews 10:25, God's Word Translation).

For this reason, the Apostle Paul encourages us to put on the FULL ARMOR OF GOD and to REMAIN STANDING. In Ephesians 6:10-13 (NLT) he declares, "[10] A final word: Be strong in the Lord and in his mighty power. [11] *Put on all of God's armor so that you will be able to stand firm against all strategies of the devil.* [12] For we are not fighting against flesh-and-blood enemies, but against evil rulers and authorities of the unseen world, against mighty powers in this dark world, and against evil spirits in the heavenly places. [13] Therefore, put on every piece of God's armor so you will be able to resist the enemy in the time of evil. *Then after the battle you will still be standing firm.*"

We've got to remember that even though the Devil uses storms to try to take us out, he has no authority, no dominion over us, and no legal right to carry out his plans. Isaiah 54:17 promises, "No weapon formed against us shall prosper..." Genesis 50:20 encourages us to understand that what the enemy meant for harm God will use to bless us and to bless others, so that we can impact them with our lives. Revelation 12:11 declares, "And they overcame him [Satan] by the blood of the Lamb and by the word of their testimony..." I want you to know that you have a testimony that if shared with the world, can make a huge difference in their lives.

As God's children, we were never meant to break or to collapse under the pressures of storms. We were meant to weather them, to overcome them, and to become experts at casting all of our cares on God. God's plan has always been that we would allow Him to be our refuge and our strength. It is His job as our God, to bring us out unscathed and to deliver us more empowered in our faith and confidence in His unfailing love.

Psalm 92:12 (AMP) states, "The [uncompromisingly] righteous shall flourish like the palm tree [be long-lived, stately, upright, useful, and fruitful]; they shall grow like a cedar in Lebanon [majestic, stable, durable, and incorruptible]."

Do you see that? That is how God sees us. We are the Righteousness of God in Christ! Our Heavenly Father has promised, "With long life I will satisfy him/her, and show him/her My salvation." Salvation is wholeness, perfect soundness and Blessing in every area of our lives. It is wholeness in our finances, in our health, in our relationships, in our mind, in our will, in our emotions, and in our desire to follow and to serve Jesus. He has commanded that everything concerning us will be fruitful, Blessed, and prosperous IN HIM. He has promised that we will stand sturdy and tall like the majestic cedars of Lebanon. An amazing thing about the Cedars of Lebanon is that those trees would reach heights of up to 130 feet tall and about 45-50 feet in circumference. What a symbol of our power and our majesty in Jesus—don't you think? If God sees us as a Cedar of Lebanon, don't you think it's time to quit seeing ourselves as grasshoppers and begin seeing ourselves the way He sees us? (See Numbers 13:33). I certainly do!

Allow the palm tree to become a model for your faith today. Learn to gently bend under the pressures of each storm you face, but do it without breaking. Decide to drop all of your baggage, all of your cares and concerns, and cast them over onto God. Then choose to surround yourself with people of like precious faith. Surround yourself with people who will help to build you up and people who will hold your hands when you are experiencing adversity. Connect with people who will be there for you when the winds of life begin blowing your way. You were meant to weather the storms of life and to stand tall and victorious after they have passed you by. You're more than a conqueror in Christ Jesus, so STAND FIRM IN HIM!

Daily Declaration

I declare that I am the righteousness of God in Christ Jesus. I am more than a conqueror in Him. I decree that no weapon formed against me shall prosper. When the Devil mounts an attack against me, he will flee from me in seven directions (Deut. 28:7). I have cast all of my cares onto God because He loves me. He is my God. Even though I know that the storms of life will try to come my way, I am convinced by God's Word that I will remain victorious in Jesus. His is my rock and my foundation. I declare that in Him I live and move and have my being. Devil, I bind you in the name of Jesus! You have no authority in my health, in my finances, in my career, or any other part of my life. I am Blessed and empowered to prosper in all things, in Jesus.

He has given me the authority in His name to cast out demons, to speak in new tongues, to lay hands on the sick and they will recover. (See Mark 16:17-18). I declare that I walk in all of the authority that Jesus has made available to me. I am an overcomer in Him! I pray all these things in the name of Jesus, Amen.

Day 10

Declaring War On Fear

"Fear not [there is nothing to fear], for I am with you; do not look around you in terror and be dismayed, for I am your God. I will strengthen and harden you to difficulties, yes, I will help you; yes, I will hold you up and retain you with My [victorious] right hand of rightness and justice."

Isaiah 41:10 (AMP)

I absolutely despise fear! I don't care how many times you have heard psychologists, doctors, or motivational speakers tell you things like, "a little fear is good for you," it is a lie! The truth is that fear will KILL YOU, if you don't get rid of it. Fear is a demonic spiritual force, which will take more and more ground in your life, if YOU do not eradicate it with the Word and faith. Just as faith comes by hearing the Word of God, Fear comes by hearing—hearing the lies of the Devil and then through meditating on and believing those lies.

2 Timothy 1:7 (NKJV) declares to us, "For God has not given us a spirit of fear, but of power and of love and of a sound mind." Power, Love, and a Sound Mind are all good things; they are all connected to the character and Spirit of God. The word which is translated in English as "power," is the Greek word *Dynamis*, which

literally means: to possess supernatural, Holy Spirit, ability. The word translated as "love" here, is the Greek word *Agape*, which refers to the unconditional, God-kind of love which is not based on anything other than the character of God who **IS LOVE**. And finally, the word which is defined as having a "sound mind," comes from the Greek word *Sophronismos*, which means: to have a self-controlled mind, which is free from the control of another.

So what does all of this mean to us? God is telling us through the Apostle Paul, that we are to not be timid or intimidated by the threats made to us by the devil. Satan is always seeking for a way to gain access and ultimately control of our lives. His primary method is through suggesting negative thoughts, which are designed to cause us anxiety, and then lead us into worry and fear. Paul is telling us that fear is never given to us by God, but it is subtly suggested to us by the devil. Fear, worry, and doubt are all designed to give Satan a legal access point into our lives—because fear is a sin. Romans 14:23 tells us, "For whatever is not from faith is sin." Fear is actually the opposite of faith; it is faith in the wrong or opposite direction. So when fear tries to barge its ugly self into our lives, we should reject it altogether. When fear tries to rush in and take over, we need to cast it down (See 2 Corinthians 10:5), and recognize that God loves us and that He will never leave us or forsake us.

One of my all-time favorite Bible verses that helps me remember God's faithfulness is Hebrews 13:5-6 (AMP) which says, "[5]...For He [God] Himself has said, I will not in any way fail you nor give you up nor leave you without support. [I will] not, [I will] not, [I will] not in any degree leave you helpless nor forsake nor let [you] down (relax My hold on you)! [Assuredly not!] [6] So we take comfort and are encouraged and confidently and boldly say, The Lord is my Helper; I will not be seized with alarm [I will not fear or dread or be terrified]. What can man do to me?"

We have already seen from Hebrews 13:5-6, that God will never leave us or forsake us. But there are two additional Scriptures which prove this same truth. In Deuteronomy 31:6, 8 we read, "⁶ Be strong and of good courage, do not fear nor be afraid of them; for the Lord your God, He is the One who goes with you. He will not leave you nor forsake you...⁸ And the Lord, He is the One who goes before you. He will be with you; He will not leave you nor forsake you; do not fear nor be dismayed." (See also Joshua 1:5).

In 1 John 4:18 we learn the true nature of fear—it is a device which is meant to torment us. "There is no fear in love [who is God]; but perfect love [*Agape*—the God –kind of love] casts out fear, because fear involves torment. But he who fears has not been made perfect [has not matured] in love [who is God]."

God has nothing to do with fear. He abhors fear. Fear cannot remain in His presence. Why? Because fear brings with it, the spiritual characteristics of Satan, the force of torment, hate, and bondage! Torment is the unrelenting state of being in perpetual misery. Noah Webster's 1828 Dictionary states that the word torment is derived from English word *Tour*, which deals with twisting and straining miserably in either body or mind.

Think about it for a moment. Satan continually twists the truth of God's Word. He is the Father of all lies. The Devil continually tries to torment people with the ideas that they are going crazy, that they are going to fail, that they are going to remain sick, or that they are going to die—but these are all lies, **UNLESS YOU ACCEPT THEM**. The way that you accept them is by receiving those fearful thoughts, by meditating on them, by speaking them out of your mouth, and by acting on them as the truth for YOUR life. Don't do it—Cast down those imaginations—those thoughts and false images which Satan tries to convince you to receive through fear! (See 2 Corinthians 10:5).

Declare war on fear today! Every time the enemy begins twisting the Word of God and trying to convince you that you are destined to fail, to fall short, or to die, tell him what God has said about you! Preach the Word to him, and tell him that you're not having what he's dishing out! Let him know that you have drawn a line in the sand and that he has crossed that line. Tell him that he is in for a good whipping by your Savior and Big Brother Jesus for over-stepping his boundaries. Then remind him that he is a liar and that your Heavenly Father has commanded you to FEAR NOT! That He has ordered you to be courageous, and to recognize the truth that He will NEVER leave you or forsake you! Remind that scheming devil that God has MADE YOU to BE Victorious and safe, in palm of His right hand.

Finally, remind that lying snake that Isaiah 59:19 says, "When the enemy comes in like a flood, The Spirit of the Lord will lift up a standard against him." What is that standard? It is a big banner that tells him that you are off limits to all of his schemes and devices. It is a Holy Ghost sign that reminds him that he better flee, or risk the wrath of God. Believe me; the devil doesn't want any more torment than he is already experiencing.

Jesus whipped Satan on the cross. He made a show of him in Hell, and He is rubbing his nose in it night and day by using us as His hands and His feet in the earth. The Devil knows that the day is quickly approaching when he will be locked up in Hell forever. Remind the Devil of that, and then begin to rest in the Power, Love, and Soundness of Mind which has been given to you by your Father—You Are an Overcomer In Jesus—You overcome him by the Blood of The Lamb (Jesus) and through the Word of your testimony—What You have to say about it matters. You have been set free from the power of fear, worry, doubt, shame and torment, in Jesus' mighty name! And WHOM THE SON SETS FREE is FREE INDEED! (See John 8:36).

Daily Declaration

In the name of Jesus, I declare war on fear! I declare that I am FREE from every form of fear, worry, doubt, shame, and torment! Jesus has released me from the Curse of fear by being my Lord and Savior. I receive the Love of my Heavenly Father and I think only on those things which are true, noble, just, pure, lovely, of a good report, and those things having virtue and a praiseworthy nature. (See Philippians 4:8). I am confident that my God will always be there for me when I need Him. My job is to seek Him, to feed my spirit with His Word, to continually operate from a position of faith, and to reject and cast down every thought that is contrary to His promises in the Bible. I am Blessed in my thinking, Blessed in my speaking, and Blessed in all of my doing, in the name of Jesus. Heavenly Father, I repent for all of my sins against you. I ask you to forgive me for my sins, in the name of Jesus, my High Priest and Lord. Father your Word says in 1 John 1:9, that when I confess my sins, you are faithful and just to forgive me of my sins, and cleanse me from all unrighteousness. I receive my forgiveness now by faith, in the name of Jesus! Fear you have no place in my life or in any of my circumstances! I bind you Satan, and I break every stronghold that you are trying to set up in my life! I slam every door shut that I have knowingly or unknowingly opened up to you in the name of Jesus. And I command you to Flee now in Jesus name! I declare my life, the lives of my family members, and the lives of all of those who I will influence and interact with FEAR FREE—In Jesus' Mighty name, Amen!

Day 11

I Believe That I Receive-It's Mine!

"Therefore I say to you, whatever things you ask when you pray, believe that you receive them, and you will have them."

Mark 11:24 (NKJV)

In case you are unaware, this verse illustrates the heart of God towards His Children. If we Christians could just grasp what the Lord is saying to us without qualifying it through our preconceived ideas, we would begin to live free from fear, free from lack, free from all of the junk that the enemy has tried (and succeeded in many cases), to get us to receive from him. He doesn't have anything worthwhile anyway—everything he has is contrary to the promises of God. It's all part of the Curse, and we were meant for the Blessing!

Keith Moore, one of my favorite ministers, wrote a song years ago titled, "*I Believe I Receive.*" Every time I read this verse, I want to break out and sing that song, "I believe that I receive, it's mine. According to the Word of God it's mine. I know the Lord has heard my prayer, I cast upon Him all my care, Now I know the answers here, it's mine." This song is an excellent example of real faith in God's Word. It is an example of the way that you and I need to respond EVERYTIME we go to our Heavenly Father in prayer asking for healing, finances, for healing in our relationships and marriages, asking for the protection and well-being of our children, or for our businesses. Whatever we are praying for, we need to present His Word concerning those things, and then receive them right then by faith. Faith takes possession of what it has asked for, the instant that the prayer is made. The next step is to thank Him for providing the thing that we requested of Him. We say something in line with that song and give Him praise for His faithfulness.

Look at Mark 11:24 again, "Therefore I say to you, whatever things you ask when you pray, believe that you receive them, and you will have them." What did Jesus say? He said *WHATEVER THINGS* you ask for *WHEN YOU PRAY*…Jesus didn't limit the things that we could ask Him for! No, He left it up to us. He left it up to whatever we could believe Him to give us. He is saying to us, "It doesn't matter what you need I AM able and willing to provide it for you." Jesus didn't say, "You can ONLY pray for and have the things that the people in your church can believe me for." He didn't say you can pray for healing, for the salvation of your loved ones, or for little tiny things, and then I'll decide which one's I'll give you and which ones I won't." No, Jesus said *WHATEVER THINGS*—that leaves it completely open to the size of our faith in Him.

Jesus continued by clarifying our part in the prayer process, "…*Believe* that *you receive them*, and *you will have them*." When are we supposed to believe that we receive them? We believe that we receive those things that we have prayed for the moment that we ask Him for them. That is when we take possession of them by faith. "But how do we do that you may ask?" We do it the same way that we take ownership of a new home or a new car when we purchase it via credit or by loan. Is that car or home paid off, the moment that we drive it off of the lot, or the instant that we begin moving our furniture into it? No, but we immediately begin painting walls, decorating it the way that we desire. We hang curtains in the windows or place stickers on our bumpers. We even begin receiving mail at our new address and we invite friends over to visit our new home, yet it hasn't been completely paid off. We even begin showing and telling everyone that those things belong to us.

Why would we do such a thing? We do it because we know how the system works. We know what the contract has to say about that car or that house, and we understand the binding covenant agreement which dictates that those things belong to us unless we fail to do our part in upholding that covenant agreement! Faith to receive answers to our prayers works exactly the same way, but the good news is that Jesus paid our debt in full. The only things that we have to do, is to reap the benefits of those things that He has provided for us. We are responsible to receive Him as our Lord, and to obey and believe His promises in the Bible. The Bible is the covenant agreement and it has been signed with His death, His blood, and with our confession of faith IN HIM!

Now look with me at Hebrews 11:1 (AMP) which expresses the same truth that I just shared above, "Now faith is the assurance (the confirmation, the title deed) of the things [we] hope for, being the proof of things [we] do not see and the conviction of their reality [faith perceiving as real fact what is not revealed to the senses]." Faith is not based on what we see. Faith is based on what God has promised to us! If God has said that something belongs to us in His Word—then we can BELIEVE Him and take possession of that thing by faith.

1 John 5:14-15 (AMP) explains this prayer process with more clarity, "[14] And this is the confidence (the assurance, the privilege of boldness) which we have in Him: [we are sure] that if we ask anything (make any request) according to His will (in agreement with His own

plan), He listens to and hears us. [15] And if (since) we [positively] know that He listens to us in whatever we ask, we also know [with settled and absolute knowledge] that we have [granted us as our present possessions] the requests made of Him." Wow that is amazing! We are sure…we know with settled and absolute knowledge…that we HAVE what we have asked for! That leaves no room for any doubt if you ask me!

You may still be asking yourself the question, "How do I know whether or not what I am asking for, is within His plan?" Let me answer your question. Can you find the promise of it made to you anywhere in the Bible? If you need healing in your body, all you need to do is to look at all of the people that Jesus healed. How many people did the disciples pray for or lay hands on, that were healed? If you want to be free from fear, anxiety, worry, or guilt, there are at least 365 Scriptures which command us to fear not, to be courageous, or that tell us that God has not given us the *SPIRIT of FEAR*. Find your promise in the Bible and take possession of what you want by faith. A good rule of thumb is to find a minimum of at least three Scriptures that illustrate that healing, freedom from fear, or prosperity belong to us, through our covenant relationship with Jesus.

I know that there are a great many things that we pray for besides healing and deliverance from fear, but there are Scriptural promises for those things too. Philippians 4:19 (AMP) states, "And my God will liberally supply (fill to the full) your every need according to His riches in glory in Christ Jesus." Psalm 37:4 declares, "Delight yourself also in the Lord, and He will give you the desires and secret petitions of your heart."

2 Peter 1:3-4 promises us, "[3] His divine power has given to us all things that pertain to life and godliness, through the knowledge of Him who called us by glory and virtue, [4] by which have been given to

us exceedingly great and precious promises, that through these you may be partakers of the divine nature, having escaped the corruption that is in the world through lust." Those three Scriptures alone cover all of our needs and all of the desires that we may have, which are not specifically mentioned by name in the Bible—Isn't God Good?

I would encourage you the next time you pray to physically reach out in front of you with your hand, to grasp for and to close your hand around the thing you are asking Him for. As you do this exercise of faith, pull that thing back towards you as a symbol of taking imme-diate possession of it. Remember that this is an act of your faith! Don't allow the devil to say one word in opposition to what you are believing for. The moment he opens his ugly mouth, tell him to shut up, in Jesus' name!

Remind him what James 4:7 says, "Submit yourselves there-fore to God. Resist the devil, and he will flee from you." If you have made Jesus the Lord of your life, then you have submitted to his authority and Lordship. Let the devil know that you are resisting all of his lies, all of his doubt and unbelief, and all of his deception—and remind him that his job is to flee from you! Then start singing, "I believe that I receive, it's mine. According to the Word of God it's mine. I know the Lord has heard my prayer, I cast upon Him all my care, Now I know the answers here, it's mine." Rub your unwavering faith in the Devil's face and take possession of all that God has prom-ised to you, in Jesus, AMEN!

Daily Declaration

I declare that I am a person of great faith. I have world overcoming faith which is pleasing to God. My faith is so great that it can move mountains and receive the answers to "impossible" circumstances. The Bible promises me in Mark 9:23 that, "If I can believe, all things are possible to me because of my belief." In Matthew 17:20 Jesus said, "For assuredly, I say to you, if you have faith as a mustard seed, you will say to this mountain, 'Move from here to there,' and it will move; and nothing will be impossible for you." And in John 11:40 Jesus promised, "Did I not say to you that if you would believe you would see the glory of God?" I declare that I am a Believer, not a doubter! I declare that the devil is a liar and I choose to reject any and everything that he would try to convince me to believe. The Bible is my foundation and my standard for life. I have what the Bible tells me I have, I can do what the Bible says I can do, and I am what the Bible says that I am, in Jesus' name, Amen.

Day 12

Your Abundance Begins With You

"[18] The Spirit of the Lord is upon Me, because He has anointed Me to preach the gospel to the poor; He has sent Me to heal the broken-hearted, to proclaim liberty to the captives and recovery of sight to the blind, to set at liberty those who are oppressed; [19] to proclaim the acceptable year of the Lord."

Luke 4:18-19 (NKJV)

I find it interesting that the Lord finds hardship, lack, insufficiency, and poverty ALL unacceptable, but for some reason, many of His children sees them as being His will for their lives, or as a symbol of true holiness, or the fruit of real Christianity.

The Bible instructs us that we are to have the mind of Christ (1 Corinthians 2:16). God's Word tells us that we are to align or renew our thinking to match His way of thinking (See Romans 12:2). In 2 Corinthians 4:3-5 we read, "[3] But even if our gospel is veiled, it is veiled to those who are perishing, [4] *whose minds the god of this age has blinded, who do not believe*, lest the light of the gospel of the glory of Christ, who is the image of God, should shine on them. [5]For we do not preach ourselves, but Christ Jesus the Lord, and ourselves your bondservants for Jesus' sake."

For those of us who teach about the Biblical nature of Godly prosperity, we believe that it is paramount for God's people to understand that prosperity is living free from the curse and bondage of sin. We want people to know that it is not God's will for His people to remain in any state of lack. Sickness is caused by the lack of healing in one's body. Poverty is caused by the lack of wholeness in a person's finances. Destructive or abusive relationships are the result of the lack of love and compassion. I think you get the idea here. Jesus has given us the keys to FREEDOM from lack and dis-ease. But religion, man's traditions, and incorrect understanding of God's true will for all of humanity has taught that poverty is a noble and holy thing.

If that were true, then why are we all fighting against God? Why are we all trying to prosper and to succeed in life? Why don't we just quit fighting Him and lie down and die? I know it sounds silly, but that is exactly what many of God's people have allowed Satan to convince them of. They have allowed him to convince them that having good things is somehow wrong or evil. But if good things are so evil then give up your home. Give up your nice clothes. Give up your desires to go on enjoyable vacations and just go live out at the dump and scavenge for rotten and putrid food! The reason we don't do this is because we don't really believe that it's God's will for us to live that way. If we did we would be going against the will of God for our lives—Right? Do you see that?

The truth is however, that prosperity is not just about money. Prosperity is ALL-INCOMPASSAING. Prosperity deals with your spirit, your health, your relationships, your material needs and your desires. Prosperity involves every aspect of who man is: spirit, soul, and body. And in reality, prosperity begins with what YOU BELIEVE!

Think about it this way: ANYTHING that is too BIG or too much for YOUR faith, is forever out of YOUR reach! You MUST BELIEVE that ABUNDANCE is a part of YOUR God-given inheritance, or YOU will never experience it! You have to receive ALL of YOUR inheritance IN CHRIST (perfect health, joy, wealth, Blessed children, a great career, a great marriage, more than enough, etc.), or you will only live in, and enjoy a portion, of the "precious promises," which God has made available to you IN JESUS.

The Blessing of God all started back in Genesis 12:1-3 with God's covenant man Abraham. When God said to him, "Abram: "Get out of your country, from your family and from your father's house, to a land that I will show you. *² I will make you a great nation; I will bless you and make your name great; and you shall be a blessing. ³ I will bless those who bless you, and I will curse him who curses you; and in you all the families of the earth shall be blessed.*" (Emphasis Added).

God had to get Abram away from the people who would hold him back or be a stumbling block for his faith, because of their false religious ideas, their unholy traditions, and because of the lack of commitment to the One True God, through their worship of many idols. The same is true for us. We must decide for ourselves that God's Word is the final authority for our lives. If the Bible says it, and if we have a minimum of two or three witnesses to that truth, then we are to believe it, and to shape our lives around that truth. An example would be to understand that it is God's will for us to be healed (See Exodus 15:26, Psalm 103:1-5, Psalm 107:20, Isaiah 53:4-5, Matthew 8:17, 1 Peter 2:24, and 3 John 2).

God was also telling Abram, "I want you to leave all that you know, all that you have relied upon to make it in this world, and I want you to begin to understand that I am now your source. I want you to understand that—I AM whatever you need me to be, that I am El Shaddai—YOUR God of more than enough.

Did you know that it was God's will for The BLESSING to transfer from generation to generation? It was His will to take care of each person who belonged to Him. Look at Genesis 25:5-6, 11 (NKJV), "And Abraham gave all that he had to Isaac. [6] But Abraham gave gifts to the sons of the concubines which Abraham had…[11] And it came to pass, after the death of Abraham, that God blessed his son Isaac. And Isaac dwelt at Beer Lahai Roi (The well of the Living One who sees me). God is always mindful of all of His children. The name of that well reminds me of another name for God—Jehovah Jireh or Yahweh Yireh. In English, we understand this name for God as being The Lord God my provider, but the literal Hebrew means the God who sees beforehand and therefore provides. God knows what you need before you do and He is willing to give it to you, at just the right time, as long as He is YOUR GOD. As long as you have made Him YOUR SOURCE by receiving Jesus as YOUR LORD.

Just to prove this point from Scripture, look with me at Genesis 27:27, 41. Here we see that the Blessing of God being transferred from Isaac to Jacob, "[27] And he came near and kissed him; and he smelled the smell of his clothing, and blessed him and said: "Surely, the smell of my son is like the smell of a field which the Lord has blessed…[41] So Esau hated Jacob because of the blessing with which his father blessed him…" Esau understood that the Blessing which was pronounced over his brother was real, and that it was to be esteemed.

Finally, in Galatians 3:13-14, 29 (NKJV) we read, "[13] Christ has redeemed us from the curse of the law, having become a curse for us…[14] that the blessing of Abraham might come upon the Gentiles [the nations, those who are not Jewish by blood], in Christ Jesus, that we might receive the promise of the Spirit through faith…[29] And if you are Christ's, then you are Abraham's seed, and heirs according to the promise."

Please understand and receive by faith the truth that the promise of the BLESSING which originated with Abraham, also belongs to you, because of your relationship with Jesus as YOUR Lord and Savior. We are Heirs, you and I have an inheritance, and God isn't handing out junk. He is handing out the BLESSING—the freedom from every type of spiritual, physical, and material lack which exists. But in order to start on YOUR journey to a life of abundance, you must come to the place of understanding, believing, and receiving it by faith, as belonging to you NOW! Your Blessing, Your Abundance, and Your Prosperity—ALL begin with YOUR FAITH! Understand, Believe it, and Receive it TODAY by Faith. Then begin living exceedingly, abundantly, above all, that you could ever dream or imagine—IN CHRIST JESUS!

Daily Declaration

I declare that I am free from every form of oppression, lack, and strife. I am determined to walk in love and to live in the abundance that Jesus died to make available to me. Father, I receive the Blessing which you gave to Abraham, my spiritual ancestor in the faith. I am a legal heir to that Blessing through my relationship with Jesus, and I therefore take possession of all that I am heir to in Him. I speak your supernatural favor over my mind, my health, my family, my business, my emotions, my relationships, and my finances in the name of Jesus! I call each and every one of those areas in my life BLESSED! I decree that I am free from the spirit of lack, from the attacks of the enemy, and each and everything that would try to keep me from succeeding in the destiny that you have for my life. Thank you Father for Your love and Your supernatural favor operating in my life. I truly am Blessed to be a Blessing. I declare all of these things in Jesus' name, Amen.

Day 13

How Do You Spell Success?

"Turn to the Lord for help in everything you do, and you will be successful."

Proverbs 16:3 (Easy-to-Read Version)

C ould you define what your personal idea of success looks like if I asked you to describe it? I would be willing to bet that many people would define success as having millions of dollars and being able to do whatever they wanted to do. Some might say that success would be owning a thriving business that had made them feel prosperous and influential. Yet others might say they would define success by being able to retire early and spend their lives touring the world from one luxurious place to the next.

The interesting thing is that each and every one of us would define success in our own unique way. Sure each of us would include some aspect of financial freedom and good health as part of our definition. We would also want our family members to be healthy, happy, and free from worry. But from that point forward, our personal definitions would most likely be very different from the next person's.

I don't know if you have ever really thought about it but I believe that the reason that some people enjoy absolutely amazing lives and others don't, is because they have taken the time to really define what they want in life. Once they have created their personal defini-tion, they then aim for those things purposefully, while the other group just hopes that those things will magically fall into their laps by chance. But I don't believe that we ever get to that amazing life we desire, by chance. I believe that in order to reach our definition of success, we have to meticulously outline what our picture of success looks like, and then work towards it by believing God and taking practical action steps to get there.

Proverbs 16:3 tells us that when we turn to the Lord, when we include Him in all that we do, then He will bless us and we will enjoy true success. Inviting God into our lives to help guide and direct our steps is something that I believe many Christians forget to do. For example: let's say that you meet a wonderful person and begin dating, but you never bother to ask God if that person is the right person to be your spouse. You may quickly decide to jump into a marriage, but when things begin to go south, you get mad at God and blame Him for the failed relationship. I've seen this happen over and over and then these people say things like, "Why did God let this happen to me?" Or, "How could He do that to me, I thought He wanted me to be blessed?" The truth is that God had nothing to do with it. These people never took the time to invite God into that relationship, or to ask Him if they should move forward in it. Instead they jumped in with both feet. They liked what they saw and they allowed their emotions and their lust to convince them that it was smooth sailing. They didn't bother to pay attention to the signs that warned them of turbulent tides ahead.

Besides inviting God into our affairs, I also believe that we need to pray specific prayers or we might end up with something that we don't really want. We might pray something like, "God, I pray that you bring me that perfect spouse." And after a period of time waiting patiently, we wake up one morning to find that years have passed, and we are still not any closer than we were before. Sure we may have met some pretty amazing people, but no one that quite fits our mold of, "Mr. or Ms. Right." I believe this happens because we haven't taken the time to tell God exactly what we wanted. We haven't defined our picture for ourselves or for God. We never asked Him to bring us that person with red hair and freckles. We never made the quality decision that we wanted that person to be somewhere between 5'11 and 6'2" tall. We never made it a priority that we wanted our future spouse to love hang-gliding. So as a result, God brought us every other type of person we could imagine—but not Mr. or Ms. Right. Whose fault is that?

Now I know what you're thing. "But doesn't God already know the desires of our hearts?" Yes He does, but it is still our job to ask Him for what we want. The Bible tells us that God even knows the number of hairs on our heads (See Luke 12:7). The Bible also says in Hebrews 4:12-13 that, "[12]...God is a discerner of the thoughts and intents of the heart. [13] And there is no creature hidden from His sight, but all things are naked and open to the eyes of Him to whom we must give account." But the Bible also says that we are to, "Come boldly to the throne of grace, that we may obtain mercy and find grace to help in time of need." (Hebrews 4:16). And what about James 1:5-6 which tells us, "[5] If any of you lacks wisdom, let him ask of God, who gives to all liberally and without reproach, and it will be given to him. [6] But let him ask in faith..." One of my favorite Bible verses instructs, "Delight yourself also in the Lord, and He shall give you the desires of your heart." (See Psalm 37:4). What is the prerequisite for obtaining the desires of our heart? It is to delight ourselves in the Lord, to seek, and to inquire of Him.

In order to receive the prayer results that we want; we need to be specific in our prayer requests. Specific results are the byproduct of specific requests. Philippians 4:6-7 says, "[6] Be anxious for nothing, but in everything by prayer and supplication, with thanksgiving, let your requests be made known to God; [7] and the peace of God, which surpasses all understanding, will guard your hearts and minds through Christ Jesus."

In Joshua chapter 10 we read a story about Joshua, who needed the sun to remain in the sky in order that he might defeat the Philistines. The sun was going down but Joshua boldly prayed and asked God to keep the sun shining until his enemy was defeated. God answered his prayer. We read about another bold and specific prayer made by Hezekiah, who prayed for his healing in 2 Kings 20. God answered his prayer too and allowed him to live several years longer than he was originally supposed to live. What about Joseph and Daniel who prayed and asked God for revelation in order to interpret dreams? God answered their prayers by giving them exactly what they requested of Him. (See Genesis 41 and Daniel 9). What would have happened if these great heroes of faith just prayed ordinary non-specific prayers and left everything up to chance? I'll tell you what would have happened; they would have never received the answers they wanted or needed.

Yonggi Cho the pastor of the world's largest church congregation in Seoul, South Korea told a story in one of his books "*Prayer The Fourth Dimension*," about a desk and a bicycle that he wanted when he first began in the ministry. He prayed according to the Word of God using Mark 11:23-24 as the foundation for his faith. Time passed and pastor Cho became frustrated that God hadn't answered his prayer as he had asked. He decided to go back to God in prayer and ask Him why He had not answered his prayer. God responded to him, "Because you have not told me what kind of bicycle or what kind of desk you want me to give you. If I bring you just any bike or just any desk, will that make you happy?" Pastor Cho replied, "No, I want a red Schwinn bicycle with a basket in the front to hold my Bible." He also prayed for a specific European desk made out of a specific type of wood. When He got specific in his prayer, his answer came in a very short amount of time (within a couple of weeks or so). He received exactly what he had prayed for. The same thing will happen for you, once you get specific in your prayers. Don't leave everything up to chance or you will most likely be disappointed. If you haven't defined exactly what you want God to give you, then how will you know if you ever receive it from Him?

You and I probably have different definitions for what true success looks like. But one thing is certain; we will both enjoy the success that we desire if we will invite God into everything we do, and if we will learn to be bold enough to pray specific prayers. God wants us to enjoy life! He wants to give us things that will bless us and make us happy, whole, and proud to be part of His family. Don't ever allow anyone to lie to you, or to convince you that asking God for the things that you want and desire is being greedy. Specific prayers don't turn God off—they excite God! When He hears His children pray bold specific prayers, He says to the angels around Him, "Do you see that, this person really believes that I Am God and that I can do anything that they have prayed—So I'm going to do it for them!"

God tells us to come boldly to His throne of grace (Hebrews 4:16). He says "Seek, Ask, and Knock and promises that when we do, we will find, receive, and the door will be opened to us (See Matthew 7:7). He also tells us to delight ourselves in Him and then He will give us the desires of our hearts (See Psalm 37:4). When you are sure to do all of these things get ready to enjoy your own little piece of Heaven here on the earth. Get ready to see God create Success spelled exactly the way you would spell it for yourself—Healing, Freedom From Fear, Healthy And Blessed Children, Financial Abundance, Peace, Joy, a Prosperous Business, etc. Spell it any way you want—Nothing is impossible to the person who is bold enough to ask and to believe God for their dreams—Nothing Is Too Hard For Our God!

Daily Declaration

Heavenly Father, I ask you today, to make it clear in my spirit exactly what it is that I want my life to look like. I ask you to lead and to guide me into all truth (Psalm 25:5), so that I can ask and believe You for the life that You have created for me to live. I know that You have good plans for me. According to Jeremiah 29:11 (NIV), You have promised, "For I know the plans I have for you," declares the Lord, "plans to prosper you and not to harm you, plans to give you hope and a future." I receive all that you have for me by faith. I declare that my present and my future are amazing, prosperous, and BLESSED in the name of Jesus, Amen.

Day 14

He's Promised To Do It

"And I am convinced and sure of this very thing, that He Who began a good work in you will continue until the day of Jesus Christ
[right up to the time of His return], developing [that good work] and
perfecting and bringing it to full completion in you."

Philippians 1:6 (AMP)

I pray that you receive this understanding into your spirit
from today forward: God is not finished with you and He
hasn't left you here alone to do it by yourself. God isn't
an absent God as some may believe. No! He is an ever-
mindful and loving God who has great plans for you. You
are the apple of His eye. He loves you so very much, and He wants
you to thrive even in the midst of all the chaos going on in the earth.

Jeremiah 29:11 (MSG) declares, "I know what I'm doing. I
have it all planned out—plans to take care of you, not abandon you,
plans to give you the future you hope for." Joshua 1:5-8 (NLT) states,
"⁵ No one will be able to stand against you as long as you live. For I
will be with you as I was with Moses. I will not fail you or abandon
you. ⁶ "Be strong and courageous, for you are the one who will lead
these people to possess all the land I swore to their ancestors I would
give them. ⁷ Be strong and very courageous. Be careful to obey all the

instructions Moses gave you. Do not deviate from them, turning either to the right or to the left. Then you will be successful in everything you do. [8] Study this Book of Instruction continually. Meditate on it day and night so you will be sure to obey everything written in it. Only then will you prosper and succeed in all you do. [9] This is my command—be strong and courageous! Do not be afraid or discouraged. For the Lord your God is with you wherever you go."

You were born with a purpose! You were born to be a leader! That special and perfect gift was implanted deep within your spirit when God created you. You are not here in the world by chance—you are all part of God's plan and purpose for these very days. He has called you to live in these days so that you can excel at whatever it is He has created you to do. Your part in the equation is seeking Him to find out what your calling is. Once you've done that, and once you have submitted yourself to His authority—He does the rest.

In Psalm 138:8 (NKJV) we read, "The Lord will perfect that which concerns me; Your mercy, O Lord, endures forever." The (NLT) says it like this, "The Lord will work out his plans for my life—for your faithful love, O Lord, endures forever."

Psalm 57:2 (NLT) declares, "I cry out to God Most High, to God who will fulfill his purpose for me." Do you see how special you are to God? You are a vital part of His plan and purpose in this earth. You are a gift to this entire world, just waiting to be opened. But what happens if you never discover your purpose? What will we miss out on if you never seek and discover your purpose? You are unique and one of a kind—there is not another person like you alive today. Romans 11:29 (MSG) says, "God's gifts and God's call are under full warranty—never canceled, never rescinded."

Don't allow the enemy to get you discouraged just because you're not where you thought you'd be by now—Remember, God isn't finished with you! The best is yet to come if you'll just hang in there, if you'll keep persevering and trusting Him! Zechariah 4:10 (NLT) states, "Do not despise these small beginnings, for the Lord rejoices to see the work begin."

I want you to know that God delights in the fact that you have trusted in Him and have begun to move forward in faith toward your purpose. Just keep at it and you'll reach your Promised Land—you'll reach Your Wealthy Place in Him!

Look at Hebrews 12:1-2 (NLT) with me, "Therefore, since we are surrounded by such a huge crowd of witnesses to the life of faith, let us strip off every weight that slows us down, especially the sin that so easily trips us up. And let us run with endurance the race God has set before us. [2] We do this by keeping our eyes on Jesus, the champion who initiates and perfects our faith." Praise God He is Good! He is the One who pushes us forward. He is the One who makes it happen for us, but our job is to believe and to obey.

Allow Philippians 1:6 to become your personal motto as you persevere in faith. Begin saying it over and over to yourself, as you diligently do all God has called you to do. "And I am convinced and sure of this very thing, that He Who began a good work in [me] will continue until the day of Jesus Christ [right up to the time of His return], developing [that good work] and perfecting and bringing it to full completion in [me]." Hallelujah you are on your way! Don't give up and allow the devil to cheat you out of your destiny. God is faithful! Remember, He's promised to complete the work He's started in you, but you must not get fed up and quit on Him. I want you to know that your future is Blessed—It is Good—and You impact many lives for the better. Keep persevering in faith until you take possession of all that God has for you. You are More than a Conqueror in Christ—that means you win every time—Hallelujah!

Daily Declaration

God is working in me, around me, and through me. His perfect will for my life is in operation and is blossoming more and more each day, as I follow and obey Him. In the name of Jesus, I refuse to worry about anything. I cast all of my care on Him because He cares for me (See Psalm 55:22 and 1 Peter 5:6-7). My faith is in God and He is the One who is accomplishing and completing His plan in me. I am free from every pressure of life. It is not my job to "make" anything happen; that is God's responsibility as my covenant partner and Father. Just as Philippians 1:6 (AMP) declares, I am confident, convinced, and sure of this very thing, that He Who began a good work in [me] will continue until the day of Jesus Christ [right up to the time of His return], developing [that good work] and perfecting and bringing it to full completion in [me]. I pray all of these things in Jesus' mighty name, Amen.

Day 15

Put An End To The Pesky Distractions

"No weapon that has been made to be used against you will succeed. You will have an answer for anyone who accuses you. This is the inheritance of the Lord's servants. Their victory comes from me," declares the Lord."

Isaiah 54:17 (God's Word Translation)

Have you ever been sitting outside enjoying the beautiful sunshine, when all of a sudden a group of gnats swarm about you buzzing in and out around your head? You shoo them away, but they continue to try to distract you or disturb your peace? Those pesky boogers! They'll continue for hours and completely ruin your day, wreck your attitude, and disturb your concentration unless you take care of the problem and get rid of them for good.

The same is true with the devil. He will continue to pester, distract, and try to destroy all that you are doing, unless you stop Him with the Word. But oftentimes we waste energy swatting at him like we would a gnat. We tell him to leave us in our natural human strength instead of using our God-given spiritual authority In Christ. We need to use the name of Jesus—the name above every name which is named. The Bible says about the name of Jesus: "[9] Therefore God also has highly exalted Him and given Him the name which is above every name, [10] that at the name of Jesus every knee should bow, of those in heaven, and of those on earth, and of those under the earth, [11] and that every tongue should confess that Jesus Christ is Lord, to the glory of God the Father." (See Philippians 2:9-11). There is power in His name, Praise God! And the Devil bows to it, and then flees from His presence in terror.

Ephesians 6:10-18 (NLT) admonishes us to, "[10] Be strong in the Lord and in his mighty power. [11] Put on all of God's armor so that you will be able to stand firm against all strategies of the devil. [12] For we are not fighting against flesh-and-blood enemies, but against evil rulers and authorities of the unseen world, against mighty powers in this dark world, and against evil spirits in the heavenly places. [13] Therefore, put on every piece of God's armor so you will be able to resist the enemy in the time of evil. Then after the battle you will still be standing firm. [14] Stand your ground, putting on the belt of truth and the body armor of God's righteousness. [15] For shoes, put on the peace that comes from the Good News so that you will be fully prepared. [16] In addition to all of these, hold up the shield of faith to stop the fiery arrows of the devil. [17] Put on salvation as your helmet, and take the sword of the Spirit, which is the word of God. [18] Pray in the Spirit at all times and on every occasion. Stay alert and be persistent in your prayers for all believers everywhere."

Why do we want to waste time swatting at an enemy who is already defeated, when we've been given the supernatural equivalent to "Raid Bug Spray?" The name of Jesus, The Blood, and The Word of God are the solutions to any problem the Devil will try to bring our way. If we would just think about our problems from a spiritual perspective instead of a rational perspective we would see the obvious—we have been given everything we need to Overcome in every situation. We need to use the weapons we have been given and be done with it. There's too much work that needs to be finished to be wasting time on pesky distractions.

I have a very good friend who knows that she has a mission and a ministry, however, the enemy has used distraction after distraction throughout the years to keep her from achieving her dreams and her purpose in the ministry. All of those distractions have been packaged in to look like things that are more "important" than her personal goals and desires, but they are a trick of the enemy to keep her from reaching her full potential. They are also keeping the world from receiving the spiritual gifts that she has to offer, through continual delay.

The enemy knows that if he can keep you busy "taking care of important things," you're no threat to him. Everything this woman has done while putting her ministry on hold, "was good." She has spent years caring for her ailing mother and father. She has spent years dealing with family issues and raising children. She has spent years helping others reach their goals. But all the while she has neglected the call that she knows God created her to do. All of these 'things," are all good, but they are not God's best. She has the money and the ability to pay or to ask others to take some of that responsibility off of her shoulders, but fear and pride has kept her from doing so.

I want you to know however, that as I write this, things are changing for my friend. She has become aware of the enemy's tactics. She has recognized that the enemy has kept her busy in order to keep her off task. She is now in the early developmental stages of creating DVD and CD teachings to help train people to become free from the bondage of generational curses. She understands that part of her gift is to help people to reign as kings in life (See Romans 5:17-21 and Revelation 1:6), just as God created all Believers to reign in Christ. I am so excited to see what God is doing in her life! Praise God, He is faithful!

But the truth is that none of this would have been possible for my friend, unless she realized what was happening to her. It never could have been possible unless she took the time and used her authority in Christ to stop it. In Isaiah 54:17 (God's Word Translation) we read, "No weapon that has been made to be used against you will succeed. You will have an answer for anyone who accuses you. This is the inheritance of the Lord's servants. Their victory comes from me," declares the Lord." No weapon means exactly that—No Weapon! There is absolutely NOTHING that the devil can bring against you that can stick, unless you allow it to. You have been given Supernatural authority and protective armor, but it is your job to use it. If you're not careful however, the enemy will try to distract you and you'll be too busy running here and there putting out little fires of distraction, and never fulfill your purpose. Do you realize how fearful he is of the gift you have inside of you? Satan knows that your gift will set his kingdom on fire.

I'd encourage you to take a look at your life and see where the enemy is trying to keep you from reaching your full potential. Yes, those distractions may be packaged as things which are truly "important" and you may feel like there is no one else who could possibly do those things as well as you can, but that is pride. I'm not encouraging you to shirk your responsibilities. I'm simply asking you to evaluate what you are doing to determine if those things are energy vampires, sucking the life out of you, and distracting you from the purpose for which you were created?

Once you've done that, then pray and ask for God's wisdom regarding how to get your message out to the world. Do something— don't remain stagnant! You have a glorious and rewarding inheritance of victory ahead of you. Put an end to the weapons and distractions that the enemy is using to stall you from realizing your gifts and your purpose. Put an end to the pesky distractions and move on into your VICTORY IN JESUS!

Daily Declaration

In the name of Jesus, I take authority over all of the distractions that the enemy is using to try to keep me from reaching my full potential and purpose In Christ Jesus. God has created me with numerous ministry gifts, talents, and abilities. I declare that I will fulfill my purpose and that I will be a Blessing to the lives of everyone that I meet. God's anointing is operating in me to remove the burdens and to destroy the yokes of the enemy which has kept people trapped in their dysfunction and funk (See Isaiah 10:27). Jesus said that He is the vine and that I am the branches. He said that because I remain in Him, I will bear much fruit (See John 15:5). I declare that I am bearing good fruit and that I will continue to bear even more good fruit each day as I live and move and have my being in Him (See Acts 17:28). I declare that I am increasing more and more, me and my children. I am prospering in everything that I put my hand to in the name of Jesus! I also declare that the Devil's devices, his tactics, and his weapons are harmless against me because I have put on my spiritual armor. I plead the blood of Jesus over myself, over my family, and over all of my circumstances. I declare that Jesus is Lord of my life and that His name has dominion over every demonic device. I speak the name of Jesus over my life and I command that every demon, every enemy, every ungodly attack against me is broken off of my life, business, family, and off of my finances in the name of Jesus! I love you Jesus, and I thank you for loving and Blessing me. I pray all of these things in Jesus' name, Amen.

Day 16

Your Needs Are No Problem for Jehovah Jireh

"^{24} On their arrival in Capernaum, the collectors of the Temple tax came to Peter and asked him, "Doesn't your teacher pay the Temple tax?" ^{25} "Yes, he does," Peter replied. Then he went into the house. But before he had a chance to speak, Jesus asked him, "What do you think, Peter? Do kings tax their own people or the people they have conquered?" ^{26} They tax the people they have conquered," Peter replied. "Well, then," Jesus said, "the citizens are free! ^{27} However, we don't want to offend them, so go down to the lake and throw in a line. Open the mouth of the first fish you catch, and you will find a large silver coin. Take it and pay the tax for both of us."

Matthew 17:24-27 (NLT)

I want to share something with you that I have been meditating on for a while now. Not too long ago, I was instructed by God to leave my full-time job in the pharmaceutical medical industry and to devote all of myself to full-time ministry. This was both an exciting, yet somewhat scary prospect, because I have been the main financial breadwinner in my family for the last fifteen years. My wife has spent the majority of that time finishing school and taking care of our three children. However, two years ago my wife began her career teaching second grade which has added additional income to our household and relieved a lot of pressure off of me.

I was excited about the prospect of moving into full-time ministry because that has been my greatest desire for the last ten years. Over that ten year period, I finished both my masters and doctorate degrees in ministry. I launched two churches and have led Bible studies. I have also focused on being a good father and husband, and holding down a full-time sales career. I have done all of this while believing that one day I'd be able to launch out and pursue my dream of writing books and ministering to people. It has always been my desire to teach people who they are In Christ, to teach them about God's love for them, and to make clear to them the benefits they have in Christ, now—not just in the future.

I believe with all my heart that when you do what you love, it is not work, it's just your passion at play. For example, if you are an aspiring musician, you can pick up your guitar and sit down and play for eight hours straight and it feels like you have only been playing for a short time. The same is true if you love working on cars or motorcycles. You can spend all day in the garage tinkering on an engine and time just whizzes by. That's why people often say, "Time fly's when you're having fun—because it's true.

The somewhat scary part of leaving my career was the idea of leaving a very lucrative position. I had no clue how I was going to be able to leave my job and still pay all of my bills, and other obligations. Then the fear of possibly being wrong, tried to creep its way into my spirit. "Did you really hear God, or was that just you wanting to follow your heart?" The thought of the ridicule that I would receive if I lost everything, including my home, because I foolishly stepped out to follow my dream, haunted my mind. I battled with unbelief, fear, and doubt.

The first question that we must ask ourselves when fear tries to come in like a flood is, "Do I have peace in this decision?" My answer to that question was yes, but I was allowing the unknown to cause me to worry…"What if…?" But I soon realized that if God was telling me to step out in faith, then He would also provide for ALL of my needs. God has always been my source and supply in everything. I believe that my success in sales was all due to His favor in operation in my life. He has never let me down or failed me. The biggest reason for the fear that I was feeling, was the thought of adding any unnecessary stress to my wife and children. Once she was on board however, I became resolute—and it was full-steam ahead!

I said all of that to say this: there are always going to be obstacles that try to deter us. The enemy is always working. He is always whispering in our ears, trying to move us from a position of faith into a position of fear and doubt. There are always going to be mountains that we are going to have to speak to in order to move them out of our way. God has already done all He is going to do for us in the person of Jesus. He gave us the authority to take action and to claim our victories every time! Jesus died on the cross as our perfect substitute and He restored our relationship with the Father. He gave us access to ALL that God has including: His authority, healing, prosperity, wisdom, righteousness, justification, and redemption from the Curse of the Law. He made us the righteousness of God (Romans 5:21) and declared us to be sons and daughters, kings and priests, in Him, with the authority to rule and reign over every circumstance that we face.

In Romans 5:15-17 (NKJV), the Apostle Paul explains it to us like this, "[15] But the free gift is not like the offense. For if by the one man's offense many died, much more the grace of God and the gift by the grace of the one Man, Jesus Christ, abounded to many. [16] And the gift is not like that which came through the one who sinned. For the judgment which came from one offense resulted in condemnation, but the free gift which came from many offenses resulted in justification. [17] For if by the one man's offense death reigned through the one, ***much more those who receive abundance of grace and of the gift of righteousness will reign in life through the One, Jesus Christ.***"

When a king needs a ditch dug, he doesn't do it himself, he orders one of his servants to dig it. As children of the Most High God, we are to follow suit. We have been given the authority and right to order the things that He has given to us, to BE—in Jesus' name. The Bible says, "You shall also decide and decree a thing, and it shall be established for you; and the light [of God's favor] shall shine upon your ways." (Job 22:28, AMP). In other words, we have to open our mouths and speak the Blessing. Jesus is sitting on His throne at the right hand of the Father, and He isn't coming off of it to order that the things that we need be done; are done—that is our responsibility. He will however, back whatever we declare and command in the authority that He has given to us.

Matthew 18:18-20 says, "[18] Assuredly, I say to you, ***whatever you bind on earth will be bound in heaven, and whatever you loose on earth will be loosed in heaven.*** [19] "Again I say to you that if two of you agree on earth concerning anything that they ask, it will be done for them by My Father in heaven. [20] For where two or three are gathered together in My name, I am there in the midst of them." (Emphasis Added).

Another example of our authority and power in Christ is found in Matthew 17:24-27. Peter and Jesus had just come to Capernaum, and all eyes were on them to see if they would honor the laws and customs of that area, by paying the temple taxes. Moreover, the people were questioning Peter about Jesus, to inquire about what kind of man He was. They asked Peter questions like, "Are you and your Master going to obey the Law as we do, or do you consider yourselves better than us?" Peter immediately replied, "Of course we'll obey the Law." But when Peter returned to Jesus, not knowing how they would meet their obligations, Jesus said to Peter, "Go fishing [something Peter loved to do], and in the mouth of the *FIRST* fish you catch will be a coin that will pay the Temple tax for both of us." (Paraphrase).

Do you see that? Jesus didn't grab a pole and say, "Peter come with me and watch how the Messiah gets things done." No, He said, "Peter, go fishing, RELAX a bit, and trust me! I AM completely aware of ALL our needs. I AM capable and willing to supply ALL that you need and desire, if you'll simply follow my instructions. Now, go throw a line in the water and the FIRST fish you catch will supply EVERYTHING we need." I want you to know that NOTHING is ever too big for I AM. And NOTHING is impossible for US either, if we'll just believe God and do what He commands us to do (See Mark 9:23).

I'd encourage you to continue trusting God. Don't worry about what all of the naysayers are whispering. Don't listen to the critics or pay attention to the lies of the enemy. He may be telling you that you're going to fail, but he is a liar. Kenneth Copeland has said that while he was working for Oral Robert's, Oral taught him that there are three things that we must do in order to get our prayers answered by God. 1. Always begin by sowing a seed of your faith. 2. Once you have heard the word from God on a subject, never confer with man (flesh and bone), God's word is all you need. 3. The final thing Oral instructed Kenneth to do was to get the job done at all costs. In other words, there is no such thing as a back-up plan when it comes to FAITH.

No matter what mountains you may be facing today. No matter how impossible things may look in meeting your obligations, receiving your healing, or receiving the answer to your prayers. God is WILLING & ABLE to supply all your needs and take care of you! Keep trusting Him. Keep doing what He has told you to do. And don't quit doing what He's instructed you to do until it has been completed. Our Needs Are No Problem For Jehovah Jireh—The Lord Our Provider! AMEN!

Daily Declaration

I declare that NOTHING is too hard for God or me when I operate according to the Word and according to my faith. God has made all grace abound towards me, that I always have all sufficiency in all things and have abundance for every good work. In the name of Jesus, I declare that God is my Source and that His grace is sufficient and more than enough to meet my every need. The Bible Promises me in Philippians 4:19 that, God will supply all of my needs according to His riches in glory by Christ Jesus. I believe it and I receive it by faith right now, in the name of Jesus, Amen.

Day 17

HELP LORD!

"Thus says the Lord, The Holy One of Israel, and his Maker: "Ask Me of things to come concerning My sons; and concerning the work of My hands, you command Me."

Isaiah 45:11 (NKJV)

T his is an amazing Scripture and many people have missed what God is saying here, to His people. When they have read this they have either viewed God as a genie in a bottle whom they believe they can bark out orders to and expect Him to perform on command. Or they have seen this as an incorrect translation and have questioned, "Who am I to ask anything of God, let alone command Him to do something for me. These people usually follow up with the statement, "I am just a little worm, a nobody, and a sinner." Both of these attitudes are wrong.

In Genesis 1:26 God says, "Let Us make man in Our image, according to Our likeness; let them have dominion over the fish of the sea, over the birds of the air, and over the cattle, over all the earth and over every creeping thing that creeps on the earth." You and I are not worms; we are sons and daughters of the Most High God. We have been created in His image, created to be and to act exactly as He does,

but under the authority of His Lordship. He has given us His dominion, His authority and His ability. He has Blessed us and commanded
that we should rule over everything in the earth. (See Genesis 1:26-
28).

Romans 8:17 says, "[16] The Spirit Himself bears witness with
our spirit that we are children of God, [17] and if children, then heirs—
heirs of God and joint heirs with Christ, if indeed we suffer with Him,
that we may also be glorified together." We are God's children—His
heirs with an inheritance to ALL that He owns. Everything He has; has
been made available to our use. He has given us the legal right to
declare a thing and have it become so. (See Job 28:22). Most importantly He has given us the command to share with others who don't
know Him as Lord, and to show them what they could have if they
would make Him their God.

The story of the Prodigal Son in Luke 15, is the story of our
past. We have been arrogant and unwilling to admit that we have need
of a Savior. Sin has blocked us from having a good relationship with
our Heavenly Father, and we have left the safety and security our
home with Him, to chase after our own lusts and sinful behaviors. But
what has happened? God has not given up on us! He still loves us
anyway. In fact, God has posted Lost Son/Lost Daughter reward signs
throughout the neighborhood; He's paid for ads in newspapers, on
T.V., on the radio, and even on the internet. He has also given the
reward in advance—by sacrificing Jesus Christ on our behalf. Jesus
died to remedy our sin problem. He is the only cure to the Dis-ease
that is raging in the earth called sin. Now it's up to us, to come out of
hiding, and out from under the guilt and the shame which sin evokes,
and to come back home to Him.

Look at what Luke 15:20-24 says to us, "[20] And he arose and
came to his father. But when he was still a great way off, his father

saw him and had compassion, and ran and fell on his neck and kissed him. [21] And the son said to him, 'Father, I have sinned against heaven and in your sight, and am no longer worthy to be called your son.' [22] "But the father said to his servants, 'Bring out the best robe and put it on him, and put a ring on his hand and sandals on his feet. [23] And bring the fatted calf here and kill it, and let us eat and be merry; [24] for this my son was dead and is alive again; he was lost and is found.' And they began to be merry." God has provided for and has made available to us, everything that He owns. He isn't holding anything back from us. Just like the father in this story, God gave His BEST. Moreover, He has also put All of His strength and ability at our disposal.

In Isaiah 45:11 God says, "Ask Me of things to come concerning My sons; and concerning the work of My hands, you command Me." What does He mean when He says, "YOU COMMAND ME?" He is saying, whatever you need or desire, I AM your God. I am willing to provide for you no matter what it is that you need." He is saying, "I love you, you're family—Just ask me and allow me to Help you." **He is also reminding us that our authority is released through our words just as His authority is released when He speaks.**

Jesus said it this way in John 16:23 (NKJV), "Most assuredly, I say to you, whatever you ask the Father in My name He will give you. [24] Until now you have asked nothing in My name. Ask, and you will receive, that your joy may be full." John 14:14 says, "If you ask anything in My name, I will do it." Matthew 7:7 (NKJV) says, "Ask, and it will be given to you; seek, and you will find; knock, and it will be opened to you." God is the consummate giver. He is the Blessor not the Curser.

What do all of these Scriptures have in common? They all share the same idea that when you are at home in your Father's house, all you have to do is to ask, and He will gladly supply your needs and desires (See Philippians 4:19). You may be asking yourself, "What's so special about asking in Jesus' name?" All of His authority is wrapped up in his name. Jesus' name unlocks the doors that were once barricaded because of our sin. His name opens every door to us, because He paid the penalty for sin for all mankind.

If you're married you understand the power and authority of a name. Your spouse, who shares your last name, can go to the bank and withdraw any amount of money available to the two of you. Because she shares the same last name—She has the legal right to withdraw any and everything in your account if she wants to. Jesus has given us this same legal authority to withdraw whatever we need simply by using His name. The good news however, is that Heaven's storehouses have unlimited resources.

Think about it this way. When you visit your natural Mother and Father's home, and you are hungry, all you do is ask if you can have something to eat. You don't cower in the corner begging or crying about how unworthy you are. No, you're family, and family always takes care of one another in love. In fact, when you go home, you probably don't even ask your mom or dad if you can eat something, you just reach into the refrigerator and get what you want because you know it's OK.

The Prayer of Faith works the same way. When we go to God in prayer asking Him for His help, we present His precious promises from the Bible. They are the evidence which prove that the things we are asking Him for, belong to us according to His will. The only thing left for us to do is to take hold of them by faith when we pray, believing that we have them.

When God says, "You command my hands," He is saying, "Son/Daughter, all I have is yours. You have complete and total access to all I own. Ask me and I will do it for you, because I love you!" We must remember however, that if we don't ask Him for His help, He isn't going to just barge in and take over. God is a gentleman and He honors our independence, He honors our free-will. If you've ever been on your own and have been paying your own bills for very long however, you know that independence is not all it's cracked up to be. When you were a child in your parent's home and dependent on them, life was much simpler. But there were rules that you had to obey and specific ways that things had to be done—The same is true with God. He has a Master plan for our lives, and His plan is designed to ALWAYS work.

I'd encourage you today to quit trying to live your life all on your own. Quit trying to live independent of God. Allow Him to carry the burdens you are under so that you don't have to. He's offered to take them from you and to work it all out for your good. (See Psalm 37: 5; Psalm55:22; Matthew 6:65; Romans 8:28; 1 Peter 5:7). The word Command used in Isaiah 45:11, is the Hebrew word *tsavah*, which means to lay charge to, to give command to, or to appoint.

Decide today to appoint Jesus as Lord over *All* of your life. Ask Him to help you live a Devil stomping, Bible carrying, Overcoming, Victorious Life IN HIM! Jesus is here to help you whenever you need it. He truly understands exactly what you are going through and how to help you win in life. Hebrews 4:15-16 says, "[15] For we do not have a High Priest who cannot sympathize with our weaknesses, but was in all points tempted as we are, yet without sin. [16] Let us therefore come boldly to the throne of grace, that we may obtain mercy and find grace to help in time of need." He's here to help, but we must be willing to cry out—HELP LORD!

Daily Declaration

Father, I humble myself before you today and submit to Your authority and Your ways. Lord, Your Word declares that Your thoughts are higher than my thoughts and Your ways are higher than my ways (See Isaiah 55:8-9). The Bible tells me that there is a way that "seems right," unto man, but that it leads to sure destruction. (See Proverbs 14:12 and Proverbs 16:25). Heavenly Father, I know I need Your help today and every day. I ask You for Your Help right now, in the name of Jesus. God you have promised that when I humble myself before You, You will exalt me (See James 4:10 and 1 Peter 5:6). You have said that the Battle is Your's and the Victory is mine. (See 1 Samuel 17:47 and 2 Chronicles 20:15). Thank You for Your protection, for Your Favor which surrounds me as a shield (See Psalm 5:12), and for Your unfailing love. Thank You for Jesus Who has promised me, "[He] came that [I] may have and enjoy life, and have it in abundance (to the full, till it overflows)." I receive the Abundant and overflowing life that Jesus came to provide for me, in Jesus' name, Amen.

Day 18

Tried In The Furnace Of Affliction

"Behold, I have refined you, but not as silver; I have tested you in the furnace of affliction."

Isaiah 48:10 (NKJV)

I want to spend some time today talking about the true character of God verses the incorrect concept that some people have of Him. Some mistakenly believe that God "puts" hardships on us to teach us a lesson, and when we read Scriptures like Isaiah 48:10, it's no wonder why some are confused. I want to assure you that our God is not a God who abuses His children. He does not use harm to "teach them a lesson." But as Genesis 50:20 describes, He will use what the enemy (Satan) has meant for harm and change it for our good, and for the greater good of all.

When we read verses like Isaiah 48:10 which say, "I have refined...I have tested...followed by negative words like affliction," our natural response is to think that God is the One Who is putting us through these difficult circumstances. But that doesn't line-up with the character of God which is—LOVE.

The Hebrew word translated refine is *tsaraph*, and it means "to make something choice" (as in quality or grade), or "to make it the best through purifying," "to smelt," "to make pure," "to refine," or "to test."

It was because of the Israelites disobedience that they went into captivity. Their bondage was rooted in their sins of disobedience and in chasing after false gods. It was their unfaithful behavior that opened up the door to Satan, who, "Comes only in order to steal and kill and destroy." (See John 10:10, AMP).

Yes, God was angered by their prostitute-like behavior and because of their rejection of His standards, but it was the Devil who brought destruction upon them, not God. God simply ALLOWED it to happen because that is what they CHOSE by rejecting His commands. He didn't CAUSE it to happen. It was their sin that brought it upon them. Sin opened up the door to the thief, and he came in and destroyed their lives. We often forget that sin always demands payment, and that payment is pain, misery, and death. (See Romans 6:23).

The word translated in English as tested, is the Hebrew word *bachar*. *Bachar* means: to examine, to make something the preferred choice, or to test by examination or watchful eye. 2 Chronicles 16:9 states, "For the eyes of the Lord run to and fro throughout the whole earth, to show Himself strong on behalf of those whose heart is loyal to Him. In this you have done foolishly; therefore from now on you shall have wars."

God is always watching. Not to punish, but to exalt, to Bless, to prosper, and to promote those who are loyal to Him. However, the result or the harvest for those who turn against Him is evil. We've already learned from John 10:10 that Satan only comes into our lives in order to steal, kill, and to destroy. The actions of those in 2 Chronicles 16:9 opened up the door for the enemy to destroy them. It was their willful rejection of God's ways that led them into war—thier refusal to obey God was the cause, and war was the effect.

The good news is however, that our God is The Master Problem Solver. He often uses the enemy's devices to draw us back to Him. Some people think that just because He uses those negative circumstances and trials to draw us back to Him, that it must mean that He caused them—but that's just not true! When we come back to Him, He Blesses us like the father Blessed the repentant Prodigal Son. That father didn't torment his already shamed and hurting son. No, He gave him the best of what he had. He clothed him in the best robe, he put an expensive and beautiful ring on his finger, and then he threw a huge feast to celebrate his son's return. We must remember that God is the Blessor and Satan is the Curser. All good comes from God and all evil from the Devil. Or said another way: Our God is a GOOD GOD and Satan is a BAD DEVIL.

An example of trials being caused by the willful rejection of God and His standards, is found in Judges 10:11-14. Here God says to Israel, "[11] ... Did I not deliver you from the Egyptians and from the Amorites and from the people of Ammon and from the Philistines? [12] Also the Sidonians and Amalekites and Maonites oppressed you; and you cried out to Me, and I delivered you from their hand. [13] Yet you have forsaken Me and served other gods. Therefore I will deliver you no more. [14] *"Go and cry out to the gods which you have chosen; let them deliver you in your time of distress."* (Emphasis Added). If Jehovah God is not your God, then that only leaves Satan. By rejecting the true God of the universe, Satan then becomes your god by default.

God isn't our problem—**WE** are usually our own worst enemies. It is our unfaithfulness towards Him that opens up the door to the enemy and to affliction. God doesn't cause the affliction in our lives, but He does allow it. He has given us the free will to either choose

Him or to reject Him. (See Deuteronomy 30:19). The Blessing is connected to our choosing God. When God is no longer around that only leaves the Curse which is connected to Satan.

The word affliction in this verse comes from the Hebrew word *oni*, which literally means: to be the cause of pain, frustration, poverty, and even misery. Affliction comes only as the result of sin and disobedience. Our God: Who is LOVE, would not, could not, cause misery in the lives of those who belong to Him. He doesn't have any of the Curse in Him. I am not saying that there isn't judgment for sin, there definitely is. He will most certainly pour out His wrath on His enemies. As John 3:36 tells us, "He who believes in the Son has everlasting life; and he who does not believe the Son shall not see life, but the wrath of God abides on him."

Ezekiel 33:10-11 shows us the heart of God. Here, God is literally begging man to turn from his wicked ways so that He can Bless him. "[10] Therefore you, O son of man, say to the house of Israel: 'Thus you say, "If our transgressions and our sins lie upon us, and we pine away in them, how can we then live?"' [11] Say to them: 'As I live,' says the Lord God, 'I have no pleasure in the death of the wicked, but that the wicked turn from his way and live. Turn, turn from your evil ways! For why should you die, O house of Israel?'"

2 Peter 3:9 (The Good News Translations) compliments these passages by saying, "[9] The Lord is not slow to do what he has promised, as some think. Instead, he is patient with you, because ***He does not want anyone to be destroyed, but wants all to turn away from their sins.***" (Emphasis Added). God wants us to choose right—to choose Him, and to choose His ways, so that we can live under His protection, and His Favor, and so that we can be kept out of harm's way.

Paul testified in 2 Timothy 3:10-11 of God's unfailing mercy and grace which delivered him time and again, "[10] But you have carefully followed my doctrine, manner of life, purpose, faith, longsuffering, love, perseverance, [11] persecutions, afflictions, which happened to me at Antioch, at Iconium, at Lystra—what persecutions I endured. *And __out of them all__ the Lord delivered me*." (Emphasis Added).

In this life we will submit to one of two kingdom systems: either to the Kingdom system of Almighty God or to the World's system which is operated by Satan. There are only two choices—there is no in-between. Our words, our actions, and our allegiance to either Jesus or to the god of this world, determines our outcome. We will have to make the choice for ourselves, God won't do it for us. He has made it our responsibility to either choose Him or to reject Him. If we choose Jesus, we receive the Blessing. If we choose Satan and reject Jesus, then we are choosing the Curse and ultimately spiritual death.

The thing for us to remember is that no matter which system we choose, we will experience trials in this life because sin and Satan are real threats. But as Paul said in 2 Timothy 3:10-11, when we choose God we still encounter trials, but He delivers us out of them **ALL**! Jesus is our Victory! He is our Lord and Savior. He is our Prince of Peace and Salvation. Hallelujah!

Jesus said in John 16:33 (NLT), "Here on earth you will have many trials and sorrows. But take heart, because I have overcome the world." He also said in Matthew 5:45 regarding our Heavenly Father, "For He makes His sun rise on the evil and on the good, and sends rain on the just and on the unjust." Both good and evil occur in this world because both exist in it. God is a good God and Satan is a bad Devil.

Many people use the life of Job to try to suggest that God puts burdens, trials, and even sickness upon people to teach them spiritual lessons. What they fail to realize is that God didn't tell Satan to afflict

Job. Satan came to the throne of God suggesting that if He took away the hedge of protection which was surrounding Job, that Job would curse God. All that God did was to say to the Devil in essence, "Satan, I don't need to do anything. Job has brought down his wall of protection and favor by allowing fear to operate in his life. His fear over the sins of his children; has opened up a door for you to attack him and to steal all that he owns."

God did tell the Devil however, "I forbid you to kill him." God didn't say, "Sick'em." Devil, He just pointed out that because of Job's fear and unbelief, he had already given Satan access into his life. Satan didn't need any other excuses to sneak in and harm Job. He did what he does best—he stole from Job, He killed Job's family and animals, and He destroyed Job's life for a period of about one year. When Job finally recognized that his fear was the root of his problem, he corrected what he was thinking and speaking; and God gave him twice the Blessing that he had before all of his trials began.

Job said, "He knows where I am going. And when he tests me, I will come out as pure as gold." (See Job 23:10, NLT). Job knew he was experiencing Hell, but because he was a righteous man who was faithful to God, he also knew that God would be faithful to him. I heard one preacher say it this way, "It is true that God opens up doors that no man can shut and He shuts doors which no man can open, but there is oftentimes a lot of Hell in the hallways."

We've got to understand that trials, trouble, and affliction are all part of this life. Affliction comes because of sin and disobedience. The enemy is continually looking for opportunities to creep into our lives and to steal, to kill, and to destroy all that we have. Our job is to recognize the areas where we have missed the mark and immediately repent for those sins. Then when we cry out for God's help, we will experience what Psalm 34:17-19 promises. "[17] The righteous cry out, and the Lord hears, and delivers them *out of all their troubles*. [18] The Lord is near to those who have a broken heart, and saves such as have a contrite spirit. *[19] Many are the afflictions of the righteous, but the Lord delivers him out of them all*." Our God is a saving God, not a god who harms His loved ones. You may feel like you're being tried in the furnace of affliction, but if you will seek the Lord, repent for your sins, and cry out for His mercy, God will sweep you up and return you into His merciful graces.

Daily Declaration

I declare that my Heavenly Father is a GOOD GOD! I understand that his desire for me is to live and to thrive in the BLESSING. Father, I thank you for your unfailing mercy and grace on my life. I receive all of the good that you have provided for me by faith in Jesus. I recognize that all bad, all evil, and all destruction is caused by my sin and disobedience to Your Word. I understand that my sins open the door to the enemy. Father, I repent for all of my sins in the name of Jesus. I ask you to forgive me and to reinforce the hedge of protection around my life, my family, my business, and my finances. I declare that I am strong in the Lord and in the power of His might (See Ephesians 6:10). I decree that no weapon formed against me shall prosper (Isaiah 54:17). A thousand may fall at my side and ten thousand at my right hand, but no harm shall come near me, my loved ones, my circumstances, or my possessions, in the name of Jesus! (See Psalm 91:7, 10). The Lord gives His angels charge over me, to protect me and keep me in perfect peace (See Psalm 91:11, Isaiah 26:3, Hebrews 1:14). I declare that I am Blessed in all of my deeds! I refuse fear! I will meditate on God's Word day and night. I have fearless confidence in God and believe that He will do all He has promised. Trials may come my way, but God delivers me out of them all. I am the apple of God's eye. He takes great pleasure in me. I declare all of these things in Jesus' name, Amen.

Day 19

You Are The Architect Of Your Life: Build Something Beautiful

"You shall also decide and decree a thing, and it shall be established for you; and the light
[of God's favor] shall shine upon your ways."

Job 22:28 (AMP)

Y ou are the most important and deciding factor in YOUR life. Don't believe me? It's true! God is the most powerful being in the entire universe, but even He, cannot make you choose Him. He has given you a FREE WILL to choose either life or death Blessing or Cursing, and He will not override your willful decision.

Deuteronomy 30:15-19 (NLT) declares, "[15] Now listen! Today I am giving you a choice between life and death, between prosperity and disaster. [16] For I command you this day to love the Lord your God and to keep his commands, decrees, and regulations by walking in his ways. If you do this, you will live and multiply, and the Lord your God will bless you and the land you are about to enter and occupy. [17] "But if your heart turns away and you refuse to listen, and if you are drawn away to serve and worship other gods, [18] then I warn you now that you will certainly be destroyed. You will not live a long, good life in the land you are crossing the Jordan to occupy. [19] "Today I have given you the choice between life and death, between blessings and curses. Now I call on heaven and earth to witness the choice you make. Oh, that you would choose life, so that you and your descendants might live!" God is a gentleman; He doesn't have a gun to your head forcing you to do anything. It's YOUR CHOICE—YOU MUST DECIDE.

So many times we get stuck thinking that it is our environment, our ethnic background, our education level, and all of the other circumstances in our lives that determine our level of success in life. Yes, these things are factors that affect where we are to a certain extent, but our attitudes, our words, and our actions are so much more powerful than all of these other forces combined.

Look at Joshua 1:7-9, "[7] Only be strong and very courageous, that you may observe to do according to all the law which Moses My servant commanded you; do not turn from it to the right hand or to the left, that you may prosper wherever you go. [8] *This Book* of the Law [God's Word] *shall not depart from your mouth*, but *you shall meditate in it* day and night, that you may observe to do according to all that is written in it. *For then you will make your way prosperous, and then you will have good success.* [9] Have I not commanded you? Be strong and of good courage; do not be afraid, nor be dismayed, for the Lord your God is with you wherever you go." (Emphasis Added).

Do you see the key to your success? Your success will come from speaking, meditating, and doing what the Bible says. *Well that sounds too simple to be true Mike.* Yes, I know, but God's not trying to pull the wool over anyone's eyes—He is simply giving us the road map to get to The Blessed Life.

Now look at what the last part of verse 7 says to us. It is through speaking, meditating, and doing what the Word says to do that, ***YOU MAKE YOUR WAY PROSPEROUS AND SUCCESSFUL!*** God isn't the One who does it for you—YOU have to CHOOSE to DO IT! Success and total life prosperity (Spirit, Soul, and Body), are the bi-product of obedience to the Word of God. Success comes naturally when we do and say what the Bible says. Success is the fruit of obedience to the commands of God. It is the Fruit of the BLESSING and the FAVOR of God operating in our lives! Praise God!

Psalm 41:11 (AMP) declares, "By this I know that You favor and delight in me, because my enemy does not triumph over me." Psalm 30:5 (NLT) states, "For his [God's] anger lasts only a moment, ***but his favor lasts a lifetime!***" Psalm 5:12 (NIV) says, "For surely, O Lord, you bless the righteous; ***you surround them with your favor as with a shield.***" (Emphasis Added).

There are so many Scriptures that declare God's favor belongs to the Believer, but we must know and receive His Word as THE TRUTH for our lives if we are going to walk in it. We must choose to believe, to speak, and to appropriate His promises as belonging to us if we want to experience His DIVINE FAVOR in operation!

Read Genesis 1:26 with me. "Then God said, "Let Us make man in Our image, according to Our likeness; let them have dominion over...over every creeping thing that creeps on the earth." You have been created as an exact copy of God spiritually, and you have authority over creeps, including the devil!

Now don't take this wrong—YOU are not a god! You are a spirit who has been created to operate the same way God operates. If you have little kids, what do they do when they are young? They imitate their parents and their siblings right? Well that's what God has told us to do—to imitate Him or to act the same way He does. Ephesians 5:1 (AMP) says, "Therefore be imitators of God [copy Him and follow His example], as well-beloved children [imitate their father]."

So then how do we imitate God? We find this answer in Hebrews 11:3, "By faith we understand that *the worlds were framed by the word of God*, so that the things which are seen were not made of things which are visible." Just as God created everything that exists through the words which He spoke, we must frame our lives by speaking His Word (Bible Promises). The words that we speak matter—they matter so much in fact, that they are instruments of either life or death.

Proverbs 18:20-21 (ERV) says, "[20] Your words can be as satisfying as fruit, as pleasing as the food that fills your stomach. [21] The tongue can speak words that bring life or death. Those who love to talk must be ready to accept what it brings."

Matthew 12:37 (AMP) declares, "For by your words you will be justified and acquitted, and by your words you will be condemned and sentenced."

Proverbs 13:2-3 (NKJV) reminds us that, "[2] A man shall eat well by the fruit of his mouth, but the soul of the unfaithful feeds on violence. [3] He who guards his mouth preserves his life, but he who opens wide his lips shall have destruction."

The old Scottish nursery rhyme which declares, "Sticks and stones will break my bones, but words will never hurt me," is a lie of the devil. Just think about it for a moment. If you were ever teased as a kid or if you were ever told you were stupid, fat, ugly, or that you'd never amount to anything, you may have received those harsh statements as THE TRUTH about your identity and your future. Your belief about what was said about you could explain why you are where you are. Remember, YOU are the deciding factor in the equation—you either chose to receive what was said about you or you chose to reject it. Your beliefs, right or wrong, have framed your thinking, your attitude, and your life. They have culminated in the life you are living today?

Don't allow the lies of the enemy, the hurtful words of others, or fears that you're too old, too broke, too overweight, too whatever, to determine your destiny. Job 22:28 (AMP) gives us the freedom to choose how we will live. "You shall also decide and decree [speak loudly] a thing, and it shall be established [the foundation] for you; and the light [of God's favor] shall shine upon your ways." It's your choice—CHOOSE LIFE and build the MASTERPIECE that you and everyone else will want to live! You have been created in the image of God. You are beautiful and you are loved! BE BLESSED in the name of Jesus!

Daily Declaration

I declare that I have been created in the image of God. God has made me exactly the way that I am supposed to be. I am PERFECT in God's eyes regardless of what society might think. I declare that I am beautiful! I declare that I have the mind of Christ and that God's wisdom is leading and directing me in all my ways. I declare that I live in perfect health, in the strength and favor of God, and in submission to God's Holy Spirit. The favor of God surrounds me like a shield. Whenever people say negative things about me, their words bounce off me. I am a magnet to God's Blessing! The Curse is far from me and has no part in me. I declare that I only speak words that will bless others and bless myself. I bind negative thoughts, negative words, and negative attitudes in the name of Jesus, and I command that they flee from me now! I am building a victorious, prosperous, and healthy life by framing every part of who I am with the promises of the Bible. Where I started will not determine where I will end up. My past and my present circumstances don't determine my destiny. I speak life and Blessing to my future. I shall live, thrive, and succeed, in all that I do! God is for me and His favor is leading me into triumph, victory, and more than enough. No devil, no person, and no set-back can keep me from winning in life. I have been Blessed to be a Blessing to others. I will finish my race on top! Just as Job 22:28 promises me, "I have declared the Blessing over myself, over my life, and over my family, and those declarations have established me. The light of God's favor is shining upon all my ways in Jesus' name, Amen!

Day 20

Dare To Dream

"When the Lord restored the fortunes of Zion, we were like those who dreamed.
"

Psalm 126:1 (NIV)

Have you ever met a person that has outgrown the ability to dream? They are so stuck in the hurts of the past, and the pressures of present that they have forgotten what it was like to be a kid and to dream BIG wonderful dreams about the future. Did you know that dreams are a creative expression of our thoughts, our desires, and our imaginations? Some people have a problem with the word imagination, but our ability to use imagination was given to us by God. He gave us an imagination because frankly, He is too good, and some of the things He wants to do for us, go way beyond what we can fathom with our rational mind. That is why Paul encouraged us to believe that God can and will do, "exceedingly abundantly above all that we ask or think, according to the power that works in us." What power was Paul talking about? He was talking about the power of our imagination based on our faith in the Word of God, and backed by the Blood of Jesus.

Whether you understand this principle or not, dreams often help launch us to our next level of life and ministry. Where would Bill Gates be if he never dared to dream about creating computer software that would one day be in every home and businesses throughout the entire world? Where would Apple be, if Steve Jobs never let his creativity run wild? It was his imaginative genius that led him to see everyday people using his iPhone to access their email, to get directions, to order products over the internet, and to use apps that would help them in their everyday lives?

Dreams can inspire us to become better people. They can encourage us to believe in ourselves and to believe in God. They can even push us towards the calling that God has placed on our lives. That is exactly what happened with Gideon. "[13] And when Gideon had come, there was a man telling a dream to his companion. He said, "I have had a dream: to my surprise, a loaf of barley bread tumbled into the camp of Midian; it came to a tent and struck it so that it fell and overturned, and the tent collapsed." [14] Then his companion answered and said, "This is nothing else but the sword of Gideon the son of Joash, a man of Israel! Into his hand God has delivered Midian and the whole camp." [15] And so it was, when Gideon heard the telling of the dream and its interpretation, that he worshiped. He returned to the camp of Israel, and said, "Arise, for the Lord has delivered the camp of Midian into your hand." (Judges 7:13-15).

Not only do dreams inspire us to become better, but God uses dreams to lead us, direct us, and protect us from harm. Job 33:14-18 tells us, "[14] For God may speak in one way, or in another, yet man does not perceive it. [15] In a dream, in a vision of the night, when deep sleep falls upon men, while slumbering on their beds, [16] Then He opens the ears of men, and seals their instruction. [17] In order to turn man from his deed, and conceal pride from man, [18] He keeps back his soul from the Pit, and his life from perishing by the sword."

Both Joel 2:28 and Acts 2:17 tell us, "And it shall come to pass in the last days, says God, that I will pour out of My Spirit on all flesh; your sons and your daughters shall prophesy, your young men shall see visions, your old men shall dream dreams."

So what does this mean for us you might be asking yourself? Why should we care about dreams? I believe that dreams are one of the avenues that God will use to lead us into victory in these last days. The Bible speaks of an End-Time Wealth Transfer, where wealth will leave the hands of the wicked (unsaved people), and be placed into the hands of the righteous (those who have made Jesus Lord of their lives).

Proverbs 13:22 says, "A good man leaves an inheritance to his children's children, but the wealth of the sinner is stored up for the righteous." Ecclesiastes 2:26 (God's Word Translations) declares, "God gives wisdom, knowledge, and joy to anyone who pleases him. But to the person who continues to sin, he gives the job of gathering and collecting wealth. The sinner must turn his wealth over to the person who pleases God. Even this is pointless. It's like trying to catch the wind." And Psalm 66:12 tells us, "You [God] have caused men to ride over our heads; we went through fire and through water; but You [God] brought us out to rich fulfillment [to a place of Great Abundance]." I receive all of the abundance God is willing to give me, how about you?

If God is going to do all that He has promised to do for us, He needs people who will believe and receive BIG ABUNDANT BLESSINGS. Too many Christians that I see and talk to today are stuck in a poverty mentality. They continue to look back instead of looking forward. They are stuck looking back at their 401K or their stock losses from 2008. Instead of looking toward the promises of God and believing that He has given them the power to get wealth, health, restoration, and increase, they are focused on the negative things that have happened to them. (See Deuteronomy 8:18).

The reason that the windshield of a car is so much bigger than the rearview mirror, is because we are supposed to be spending the majority of our time looking forward instead of looking behind us. If we spend too much time looking in our rearview mirrors we will end up crashing, causing traffic jams, or both.

Life works the same way! If we want to move forward into the Blessed Life that Jesus came to provide for us, we have to dare to dream Big, God Sized Dreams. We have to be able to envision His Blessing and Goodness working in our lives, and then we must believe that we can actually take possession of those promises IN CHRIST! When are we going to start believing that we are what the Bible says we are: JOINT HEIRS WITH CHRIST JESUS (See Romans 8:16-17)? If we are truly joint heirs like the Bible tells us we are, then that means that we have an equal share in all that Jesus owns. It means that we have access to everything He has access to. It means that we need to start daring to dream bigger dreams. We need to dream bigger dreams for ourselves, for our families, for our brothers and sisters in Christ, and for those who don't have a relationship with Him yet. We need to begin dreaming for all of those who are lost and dying in this sin-filled world.

Dreams are a composite of images that scroll through our minds. They are the pictures of what could be, if we would just dare to grab a hold of them by faith. If the pictures that come into our minds don't match the Word of God—just cast them down and command them to flee in Jesus mighty name (See 2 Corinthians 10:5). Just as Philippians 4:8 tells us, we should take hold of any image, any dream, and any vision, that is true, honest, just, pure, lovely, and of a good report, having virtue, and is praise worthy. These are the type of dreams that we need to dare to dream with God.

Psalm 126:1 says that, God is trying to restore your fortunes and increase you more and more. He's trying to take you to your next level of living and into the land of abundance. He's trying to restore your health and take you into a new life marked by wholeness, a place where there is nothing missing and nothing broken. God's desire is that you and I live lives that are filled with His Blessing, but we've got to be able to dream and to receive those promises by our faith In Jesus!

Daily Declaration

I declare that I have the capacity to dream God-sized dreams. Father, I invite you to show me the things that You want me to do and to show me the things that you want me to believe you for. I am a person of Great faith. Just as the centurion said to Jesus, "Just say the word, and my servant shall be healed." (See Matthew 8:8), Lord, you say the Word and I will believe every word that you speak to me. Holy Spirit, I give You access to every part of who I am. Romans 8:26-27 says, "The Spirit also helps in our weaknesses. For we do not know what we should pray for as we ought, but the Spirit Himself makes intercession for us with groanings which cannot be uttered. [27] Now He who searches the hearts knows what the mind of the Spirit is, because He makes intercession for the saints according to the will of God." Holy Spirit speak to my spirit. Help me to see what You want me to see. I pray that the eyes of my understanding are enlightened and that I begin to learn and to believe correctly about who I am in Jesus and all that I have access to in Him. (See Ephesians 1:15-21). Father, Jesus, Holy Spirit, I declare that I am ready to begin dreaming with you, and experiencing the exceedingly abundantly above all that I can presently think or imagine. (See Ephesians 3:20). Jesus, I give you my life. Use me to bring glory to my Heavenly Father. I love You Lord, and I pray all of these things in the mighty name of Jesus, Amen.

Day 21

Stand Firm

"^{6} Now this I know: The Lord gives victory to his anointed. He answers him from his heavenly sanctuary with the victorious power of his right hand. ^{7} Some trust in chariots and some in horses, but we trust in the name of the Lord our God. ^{8} They are brought to their knees and fall, but we rise up and stand firm."

Psalm 20:6-8 (NIV)

I love people of like precious faith! They are the only people I want to be around when I'm in need of prayer, encouragement, and especially when I'm in the midst of a battle. Faith people just pump you up! I'm not talking about a bunch of hype either. Faith people won't allow you to feel sorry for yourself. They won't allow you to give up and quit. And they won't settle for anything less than what God's Word has promised to you and them. Faith people get your fire burning hotter and brighter. They help kick-start your motor and get your adrenaline pumping for the Good Fight of Faith. And they remind you that your battle has already been won. You have chosen Jesus as your Lord, and because of that, He gives you the victory as you continue to stand firm in your faith in Him.

Just the other day, I had a friend who called me just to catch up and to encourage me in my faith. The call wasn't just chit chat or small talk either. She spoke life into my spirit, encouraging me in the things that she knew I was believing God for. She prayed the Word over my life, my circumstances, and prophesied over my calling. Her words not only encouraged me, but they edified my spirit and spoke volumes more than she'll ever know this side of heaven. Man was my faith energized! I don't know about you, but when God sends people to us as instruments to confirm His Word—there's just nothing like that!

One of the things that truly Blessed my spirit was that she spoke Psalm 20:6-8 to me and reminded me that God has promised that everything is going to work out, as long as I continue to "STAND FIRM!" I knew in that instant that it was a Rhema Word from God, directly for me. I know about faith. I know about standing. I have stood for breakthroughs countless times before. But even though it may sound trivial, and even though you and I know what the Word of God says to us, sometimes we just need a loving reminder to continue doing those things that we have done throughout our walk with God. Most of us understand that standing firm in our faith even when things don't look promising, is a key requirement to getting what we want when we pray. Our prayers aren't always answered immediately. Sometimes days, weeks, months, and even years pass before we begin to see evidence that God has answered us. That said; those words that my friend spoke into my spirit were the exact words that I needed to hear right then, to push me forward in my faith.

Isaiah 7:9 (NIV) reminds us of the importance of conviction to remain standing firm during times of adversity. Isaiah writes, *"If you do not stand firm in your faith, you will not stand at all."* (Emphasis Added). Who has to do the standing? We do! Does this mean that if we don't do our part by continuing to fight the Good Fight of Faith,

continuing to believe God for our answer even when things get difficult, that we lose by default? I believe that it does. Standing is our
responsibility! However, God is faithful and there are many Scriptures
in the Bible that tell us that God will give us people to help build us up
when we're feeling weak.

In Exodus 17:8-13 (NIV) we read, "[8] The Amalekites came and
attacked the Israelites at Rephidim. [9] Moses said to Joshua, "Choose
some of our men and go out to fight the Amalekites. Tomorrow I will
stand on top of the hill with the staff of God in my hands." [10] So
Joshua fought the Amalekites as Moses had ordered, and Moses,
Aaron and Hur went to the top of the hill. [11] As long as Moses held up
his hands, the Israelites were winning, but whenever he lowered his
hands, the Amalekites were winning. *[12] When Moses' hands grew
tired, they [Aaron and Hur] took a stone and put it under him and he
sat on it. Aaron and Hur held his hands up—one on one side, one on
the other—so that his hands remained steady till sunset.* [13] So Joshua
overcame the Amalekite army with the sword." (Emphasis Added).
Praise God for good friends who help us to stand, and who help
encourage us to continue standing firm, even when the burden is too
heavy for us to remain standing by ourselves.

There is a great story in the Bible where we read about men
who cared enough about their crippled friend, that they went the extra
mile to help bring him into his healing. They wanted to see their friend
enjoying victory over his circumstances so much that they even went
to the extent of ripping apart a roof in order to get him before Jesus.
They knew that Jesus was the answer that their friend needed in order
that he might receive his healing.

It says in Luke 5:17-24, "[17] Now it happened on a certain day,
as He was teaching, that there were Pharisees and teachers of the law
sitting by, who had come out of every town of Galilee, Judea, and

Jerusalem. *And the power of the Lord was present to heal them.* [18] Then behold, men brought on a bed a man who was paralyzed, whom they sought to bring in and lay before Him. [19] *And when they could not find how they might bring him in, because of the crowd, they went up on the housetop and let him down with his bed through the tiling into the midst before Jesus.* [20] *When He saw their faith, He said to him, "Man, your sins are forgiven you.* [21] And the scribes and the Pharisees began to reason, saying, "Who is this who speaks blasphemies? Who can forgive sins but God alone?" [22] But when Jesus perceived their thoughts, He answered and said to them, "Why are you reasoning in your hearts? [23] Which is easier, to say, 'Your sins are forgiven you,' or to say, 'Rise up and walk'? [24] But that you may know that the Son of Man has power on earth to forgive sins" He said to the man who was paralyzed, "I say to you, arise, take up your bed, and go to your house." (Emphasis Added).

I love what Mark Hankins says about the men who lowered the paralyzed man through the roof so that he could receive his healing: "We all need a couple of crazy friends with radical faith, who are just crazy enough to do whatever it takes to help us get our miracle."

I'd like to encourage you to be one of those people, who has just enough radical faith, to help someone receive their miracle today. Take a moment to pray and ask God who you need to call and to lift up with a word of encouragement. Seek God and ask Him who He'd have you stop by and visit and share some Scripture to bolster their faith enough to help them to continue standing. Or cry out to God and ask Him to send you with the answer to that person who needs their miracle today. God will use any person who has a heart for Him and a heart for others. He'll use the person who is devoted and obedient to Him. Every one of us could use some crazy, radical, faith friends like that. Why don't you sow a seed of love, sow a seed of friendship, and let it all begin with you today? Be that person to remind a friend of yours that, "The Lord gives victory to his anointed." And then remind your friend that **YOU** are there for them anytime they need help to STAND FIRM! Be someone else's Blessing today in Jesus' name!

Daily Declaration

I declare that I am Blessed to be a Blessing! Father, lead me to that person or to those people who need You the most today. I am a willing and obedient vessel at Your disposal. Give me radical faith to do more than I have ever done before. I declare that You have Blessed me with more than enough. I declare that I am clay in the hands of the Master.

Use me to speak life into people, to pay a bill for someone, or to confirm Your Word to them today! Together Lord, we can change the world, one life at a time. I declare that You God, are my All in All. I declare that no matter what trials may come my way; I will remain standing In You! Father, You have declared of me in Proverbs 24:16 (MSG), "No matter how many times you trip them up, God-loyal people don't stay down long; Soon they're up on their feet, while the wicked end up flat on their faces." I am loyal to You Father. You are my light and my Salvation and I will continue to stand firm in You (See Psalm 27:1).I pray all of these things in Jesus' name, Amen.

Day 22

What Do You Need To Forgive?

"²¹ Then Peter came to Him and said, "Lord, how often shall my brother sin against me, and I forgive him? Up to seven times?" ²² Jesus said to him, "I do not say to you, up to seven times, but up to seventy times seven."

Matthew 18:21-22 (NKJV)

There is always someone that we need to forgive. Forgiveness is a tough subject especially when someone has hurt us. When we have been hurt, our flesh wants to lash out and hurt back. The unsaved mind is always concerned with getting even, but is getting even the best option for us? Of Course not! Let's take a moment to learn what the Bible has to say about forgiveness.

Matthew 18:23-35 (NKJV) says, "²³ Therefore the kingdom of heaven is like a certain king who wanted to settle accounts with his servants. ²⁴ And when he had begun to settle accounts, one was brought to him who owed him ten thousand talents. ²⁵ But as he was not able to pay, his master commanded that he be sold, with his wife and children and all that he had, and that payment be made. ²⁶ The servant therefore fell down before him, saying, 'Master, have patience with me, and I will pay you all.' ²⁷ Then the master of that servant was moved with compassion, released him, and forgave him the debt.[28] "But that servant went out and found one of his fellow servants who owed him a hundred denarii; and he laid hands on him and took him by the throat, saying, 'Pay me what you owe!' [29] So his fellow servant fell down at his feet and begged him, saying, 'Have patience with me, and I will pay you all.' [30] And he would not, but went and threw him into prison till he should pay the debt. [31] So when his fellow servants saw what had been done, they were very grieved, and came and told their master all that had been done. [32] Then his master, after he had called him, said to him, 'You wicked servant! I forgave you all that debt because you begged me. [33] Should you not also have had compassion on your fellow servant, just as I had pity on you?' [34] And his master was angry, and delivered him to the torturers until he should pay all that was due to him.[35] "So My heavenly Father also will do to you if each of you, from his heart, does not forgive his brother his trespasses."

I know that telling you that everything will be alright if you just forgive those who have hurt you, doesn't make you feel any better, and honestly, it is probably not true. The Bible tells us that in this life we will have tribulations. There are things that we will go through because we live in a fallen world. The question is however, "Are you going to decide to camp out there in your pain and self-pity, or are you going to get up, dust the dust off, and learn to love again?" Jesus has COMMANDED US TO FORGIVE! It's not a request, but a command! Forgiveness will save your life. God knew it would be difficult, but all of the important things in life usually are.

Mark 11:25-26 (NASB) explains the importance of forgiveness. In this passage Jesus says, "[25] Whenever you stand praying, forgive, if you have anything against anyone, so that your Father who is in heaven will also forgive you your transgressions. [26] [But if you do not forgive, neither will your Father who is in heaven forgive your transgressions]." God has made it plain and simple. If we want God to forgive us, we must forgive others who have hurt us. I understand that forgiveness can be difficult. I understand that it may seem unfair. I understand that it may feel impossible to think that we have it in us to get past the pain caused by another, but is it worth risking our lives over it? YOUR LIFE MAY DEPEND ON FINDING THE COURAGE TO FORGIVE.

A minister friend of mine told a story about an event that has been forever etched into my spirit. He said that he received a call form a ministry partner whose wife was in the hospital dying of cancer. This man asked my friend to come pray for his wife to be healed, and my friend agreed to come. On his way to the hospital, God told this friend, "She is being eaten up by cancer because she has been holding anger and unforgiveness in her spirit for years." God told this minister that the husband had been unfaithful when they were first married. He then told my friend, "Tell her to forgive her husband and I will heal her of that wretched disease, but if she refuses to forgive, she will die of that cancer, because her unforgiveness has connected her to Satan and the Curse."

As you can imagine, my friend didn't want to bring up the un-faithfulness which took place decades before, but in order to be obedient to the Lord, he said exactly what God had told him to say to the woman. Once he had finished saying what the Lord had command-ed, the wife began to explain that for the last 40 years of marriage she had carried around anger and disgust for her husband, because of his unfaithfulness. My friend reminded the lady what God had said, "God will heal you completely, if you will forgive your husband, but if you don't, you will die. The woman looked at my friend and said, "I will never forgive him for what he did to me." The next day she was dead.

I want you to know that it wasn't God who killed the lady; it was her unforgiveness which connected her to Satan and the Curse that killed her. Unforgiveness is a cancer in itself. It is a form of strife, and strife will burn you up from the inside out. Proverbs 26:21 (NKJV) states, "As charcoal is to burning coals, and wood to fire, so is a contentious man to kindle strife."

Carrying unforgiveness and strife is like pouring gasoline on ourselves and then lighting a match. God has forgiven us even when we didn't deserve forgiveness. Think about that! Jesus went to the cross because of you and me—because of our sin. He did it willingly however, because He loves us so much. He died so that we don't have to. Don't allow the enemy to take you out through unforgiveness. Don't allow the cancer of unforgiveness to eat you up! Forgive and walk in Victory! God will help you to forgive everyone you need to forgive. Ask Him for His help and LIVE FREE IN HIM! Jesus Is Lord!

Daily Declaration

I declare that I am quick to repent and quick to forgive others who have treated me wrong. I cast all of the pain, hurt, and the burdens that others have caused me, onto the Lord. I will not allow unforgiveness to block my Blessings. Father, I repent for any unforgiveness that I have been holding against anyone. In the name of Jesus I forgive them and I release them from any debt owed to me. I refuse to poison myself or to poison those around me, by continuing to hold onto any unforgiveness. I declare that I am FREE from the power of sin, shame, and fear! I will no longer allow fear to keep me in the bondage of pain, sorrow, or strife. God you have told me in Your Word, "The Lord is on my side; I will not fear. What can man do to me?" (See Psalm 118:6). I know that the answer to that question is that he can do NOTHING, unless I give the Devil authority by holding onto unforgiveness. I choose to forgive everyone RIGHT NOW! Thank you Lord for leading me into my wealthy place, my Blessed place, my place of healing and wholeness in Jesus! Devil, I break all of your power off of my life today! Unforgiveness, strife, and fear have no place in me in the name of Jesus! I am Free! I am Blessed! And I am Whole in Jesus' mighty name, Amen!

Day 23

Not Just Your Needs, But Your Desires Too!

"Delight yourself also in the Lord, and He shall give you the desires of your heart."

Psalm 37:4 (NKJV)

W hat is it that you want most? Is it to grow closer to God, stronger friendships, healing in your body, restoration in a strained relationship, financial increase, freedom from fear, or to spend more time with the ones you love?

All these things are possible, but there is a condition to receiving your dreams and desires. Who are you putting first? In other words, who or what is God in your life?

God wants you to BE BLESSED! He wants you to live out your dreams and desires, but He also wants you to see Him as the source for those things. He wants you to worship Him as the Creator, Giver, and Lover of your soul, and to come to Him instead of continuing to live as a Lone Ranger. You can try to be the god of your life, but you can never fill Almighty God's shoes—they're just too BIG—because He is a TOO MUCH GOD! He is a Cup Running Over God!

He is *El Shaddai*—The God of More Than Enough. And unfortunately, we are limited apart from Him.

I want to ask you to take a moment today and really worship Him. Spend some time to thank Him for your health, for your spouse, for your friends, for the finances He has already provided for you. Take a moment to thank Him for all He is in your life. Delight yourself in the truth that you serve and are loved by a BIG God who wants to lavish His love all over you.

Then take another moment to praise Him for all of the things that you are believing Him to do TODAY. Thank Him for that promotion you're believing for at work. Thank Him for debt cancellation and all of your bills paid in full. Thank Him for that healing that you asked Him to manifest in your body yesterday. Speak to your mountains, speak to your body, speak to your marriage, speak to that home you have listed for sale and command it to be sold in Jesus' name! Tell your circumstances to bow their knee to the mighty name of Jesus and to line up with the Word of God!

It may seem ridiculous to stand outside of that house that you listed, and command it to be sold NOW, in the name of Jesus! You may be thinking, "What are the neighbors going to think about me speaking to a house?" Who cares what they think? They probably already think you're crazy, because you are a Christian. Who cares what people think about you? They talk to their cars, to their plants, to their tools, and to their children all the time. They're always cursing themselves by saying things like, "This dumb car is no good, it never starts for me when I need it too." Or things like, "Look at that limb on that tree, it would be just my luck for it to fall on my roof and kill everyone." Those people speak doubt, unbelief, and the Curse over themselves all of the time and never think twice about it. At least you're speaking the Blessing!

Regardless of what the neighbors may think, I encourage you to stand there anyway and command that house to be sold for TOP DOLLAR! Tell it that you are a child of the MOST HIGH GOD and that it must listen to your voice and obey your words, in the name of Jesus! Tell that house that God has promised you the desires of your heart. Let it know that you delight yourself in God and that He has decreed His Blessing and His Favor over everything that concerns you. Let it know that you have done your part, that God is doing His part, and that it must do its part and be sold NOW! Remind that house that it will sell for the exact price that you have commanded it to, or for a higher price! I know this sounds crazy, but so does getting money to pay your taxes out of a fish's mouth. (See Matthew 17:24-27).

You have been given the keys to the Kingdom of Heaven by Jesus (See Matthew 16:19). You have been given the authority to use Jesus' name (See Mark 16:17-18 and John 14:13). The Bible tells us that we have overcome Satan through the Blood of the Lamb and the Word of our testimony (See Revelation 12:11). And we have a promise from our Heavenly Father, "You shall also decide and decree a thing, and it shall be established for you; and the light [of God's favor] shall shine upon your ways." You have the Favor of God!

Don't whisper—say what you need to say out loud, with courage, and in the God-given authority that belongs to you as a Joint Heir with Jesus! Speak to all of the mountains that are trying to stand in your way and command them to be removed and to be cast into the sea! Satan, sickness, lack, and every other part of the Curse must bow its knee to the NAME OF JESUS and to your FAITH in Him! Decree the Word of God over every situation you face. And do it believing that God will hear you and honor your words just as He honors and magnifies His Word above His name! (See Psalm 138:2). Delight yourself in Him and He will delight Himself in you! God is faithful to all of His children. Hallelujah!

Daily Declaration

I decree that my words have power. I speak words of faith, words of love, words of encouragement, and most importantly The Word of God! I understand that life and death are in the power of my tongue and that I will eat the fruit and be satisfied by the words that I speak. (See Proverbs 18:20-21). God you said that I shall decree a thing and that it will established for me. You said that when I speak Your Word, that the light and Blessing of Your Supernatural Favor will shine on ALL of my ways! (See Job 22:28, AMP). I speak life, healing, wholeness, favor, increase, and promotion, over my life and over the lives of my children! I call them BLESSED and HIGHLY FAVORED of God. I declare that they are the head and not the tail, that they are above only and not beneath, in the name of Jesus. And I command prosperity, the wisdom of God, and the Love of God over all of us—all the days of our lives! I decree that God is good to me! He has favored me and has established the work of my hands (See Psalm 90:17). The Lord takes pleasure in my prosperity and I am increasing more and more, me and my children. (See Psalm 35:27 and Psalm 115:14). God has made all grace, every favor and earthly blessing to come upon me in abundance, so that I always and under all circumstances, whatever the need, am self-sufficient in Him, possessing enough to require no aid or support and so that I am furnished in abundance for every good work and charitable donation." (See 2 Corinthians 9:8, AMP). I declare and I receive all of this in the mighty name of Jesus, Amen.

Day 24

You Are Fireproof

"²⁵ Look!" he answered, "I see four men loose, walking in the midst of the fire; and they are not hurt, and the form of the fourth is like the Son of God."

Daniel 3:25 (NKJV)

We should always pray and believe for God to keep us out of everything bad that may try to come against us. Our God is the God of deliverance, miracles, and the impossible is His specialty. God not only cares for us, but He loves us, and wants us to experience His very best. However, sometimes, our prayers aren't answered as quickly, or quite the way we want them to be. Sometimes we end up going through the fires, the floods, and the famines of life. Not because God wants us to suffer. Not because God is trying to teach a lesson as some believe, in order to draw us closer to Him. But because we have an enemy—the Devil—who is always on the prowl, looking for ways to steal, to kill, and to destroy.

Jesus told us in John 16:33, "These things I have spoken to you, that in Me you may have peace [wholeness, nothing lacking, more than enough]. In the world you will have tribulation; but be of good cheer, I have overcome the world."

A few years back there was a movie titled FIREPROOF, which starred Kirk Cameron and Erin Bethea. The two played a married couple who had gotten off track. Their marriage was falling apart and neither knew what to do to save it. They were devastated, emotionally drained, and suffering similar yet different pains and feeling rejected. Finally, Kirk's character realized that it was God's will for the couple to stay married. He began reading the Bible, walking in love, and fighting for his marriage. He was encouraged by His father to begin doing daily challenges which would illustrate his love for his wife (played by Erin Bethea). His father encouraged him to show her instead of just telling her that he loved her. He admonished him to prove to her that their marriage was worth fighting for. In his pursuit to win her back, he was motivated to express his love for her without expecting anything in return.

In the beginning of the movie, Kirk did things each day to express his love for his wife, only to have her reject them, humiliate him, and tell him that they were through. It looked as if his efforts were futile. His wife was drifting further and further from him in spite of his efforts at reconciliation. She even served him with divorce papers half way through the thirty day "Love Dare," which only hurt him more. But after much prayer, frustration, and patience (humility to continue walking in love), God brought them through the fire and the pain they caused one another, and rekindled the flames of their love. God helped them to extinguish the flames of pain and sorrow that had plagued their marriage and had almost destroyed it for good.

I don't know what kind of fire you may be going through today. I don't know if you feel swallowed by the flames of debt, impending divorce, sickness, depression, or whatever it may be. You might be feeling like you are barely hanging on. But I want you to know that just like God rescued the three Hebrew children—Shadrach,

Meshach, and Abed-Nego from the fiery furnace, God will come to your rescue too. Moreover, God has made you to be FIREPROOF!

Those flames may look like they will burn you up, but God has made it so that it is impossible for those flames to take you out. The prayers that you've prayed, asking God to deliver you from the fire altogether, may seem as if they have gone unheard. It may even look like there is no answer in sight. But I'm here to tell you, that God is going to bring you out better than when you first went into the furnace. He's going to bring you out without the slightest smell of smoke, and without even the hint of a mark on your clothes. You're not only going to survive, but God is going to make you thrive and take you to a whole new level of living in Him!

There are two things that fire can do to a person. It will either burn him/her up or it will purify and refine out all of the impurities that were once inside. I believe that some of the discomfort that you may be experiencing today; is due to the refining that is taking place inside you. God is allowing some of those things that need to be removed, to be burnt away, never to return again.

I'm not trying to insinuate that God is putting you through the fire. But the Bible does say in Genesis 50:20, that what the enemy meant for your harm, God will use and turn it into your good. Those struggles that you have been experiencing have been orchestrated by the Devil. He has been trying to take you out, but God is going to use them to take you up! God's going to use them to take you to a higher level of faith and prosperity. He's going to use them to take you to that place that you've only been able to dream about and imagine.

1 Peter 1:7-9 says, "[7] That the genuineness of your faith, being much more precious than gold that perishes, though it is tested by fire, may be found to praise, honor, and glory at the revelation of Jesus Christ, [8] whom having not seen you love. Though now you do not see

142

Him, yet believing, you rejoice with joy inexpressible and full of glory, [9] receiving the end of your faith—the salvation of your souls." Salvation does not only refer to your eternal destination in Heaven, but it also refers to your completeness, your wholeness, and the truth that you are to lack no good thing in Jesus.

If you've been fighting against the fire of divorce, God has said to you in proverbs 18:22, "He who finds a wife finds a good thing, and obtains favor from the Lord." I want you to know that God is for you and this too shall pass. If the fire you've been experiencing is a result of financial strain and stress, God has said to you in Philippians 4:19, "My God shall supply all your need according to His riches in glory by Christ Jesus." Money, resources, whatever you need, is coming your way. Keep your eyes open for your Breakthrough, because God is faithful to His Word.

God is going to bring you out and bring you through into victory, so don't give up. If the fire you are trying to extinguish has to do with sickness in your body, God has said to you Psalm 107:20, "He has sent His word and healed you, and delivered you from all of your destructions." No matter what fire, no matter what trial, no matter what obstacle you may be facing today, God has said to each of us, "If God is for us, who can be against us?"

I encourage you to hang in there until you receive the fullness of His promises. I encourage you to keep fighting for your victory, for your deliverance, for your healing, and for your freedom in Jesus.

1 John 5:4 (GWT) tells us why we need to persevere, "Because everyone who has been born from God has won the victory over the world. Our faith is what wins the victory over the world." The flames of fire that you may be facing today, may look overwhelming, but you have God's promise that He will bring you out unaffected, unharmed, and better off than you were before. Our God is a faithful God! He

never fails, and He never forsakes His people. He always keeps His Word. Continue believing Him for your victory. Keep your eyes on Jesus, the author and finisher of our faith. And continue persevering through the flames of fire—GOD HAS MADE YOU AN OVERCOMMER IN CHRIST JESUS—HE HAS MADE YOU TO BE FIREPROOF!

Daily Declaration

I declare that just as God rescued the three Hebrew children from their fiery furnace, God will rescue me out of mine. I declare that no weapon that has been formed against me will prosper in the name of Jesus! I am Blessed coming in and going out. I am more than a conqueror in Christ Jesus. The Battle is the Lord's and the Victory is mine in Jesus. I speak to the mountain of ____, and I command it to be removed and to be cast into the sea. I have Victory in every situation I face, because I choose to walk in love and to walk in faith. If God is for me than who shall dare try to stand against me? In fact, the Message Bible renders Romans 8:31-39 this way: "[31-39] So, what do you think? With God on our side like this, how can we lose? If God didn't hesitate to put everything on the line for us, embracing our condition and exposing himself to the worst by sending his own Son, is there anything else he wouldn't gladly and freely do for us? And who would dare tangle with God by messing with one of God's chosen? Who would dare even to point a finger? The One who died for us—who was raised to life for us!—is in the presence of God at this very moment sticking up for us. Do you think anyone is going to be able to drive a wedge between us and Christ's love for us? There is no way! Not trouble, not hard times, not hatred, not hunger, not homelessness, not bullying threats, not backstabbing, not even the worst sins listed in Scripture...None of this fazes us because Jesus loves us. I'm absolutely convinced that nothing—nothing living or dead, angelic or demonic, today or tomorrow, high or low, thinkable or unthinkable—absolutely nothing can get between us and God's love because of the way that Jesus our Master has embraced us." I call myself Blessed and Victorious in ALL THINGS! I pray all of this in the mighty name of Jesus, Amen.

145

Day 25

What Images Are You Allowing to Be Established In Your Life?

"And the LORD said, Behold, the people is one, and they have all one language; and this they begin to do: and now nothing will be restrained from them, which they have imagined to do."

Genesis 11:6 (KJV)

How do you see yourself? Can you picture yourself debt free? Can you see yourself on stage receiving that award? Can you imagine yourself free from pain and sickness? If you can't, you don't qualify for the promise! Those things that you are seeing and saying are the building blocks to the life that you will live.

Faith is a process of seeing and saying. People say what they truly believe about everything. Think about it for a minute. In a sense humans become pregnant with images that are either positive or negative, and then they give birth to those images, through words and actions. The negative images we call worry, doubt, and fear. The positive images we call hope, expectation, and faith. The more a person imagines and speaks in line with what they are seeing in their spirit, the more they are developing that image into their personal reality.

Take for instance a woman who has just found out that she is pregnant. Even before that child is born, she begins to imagine the future that she and that baby will share together. She begins to imagine him crawling on the ground, and his first years in school. She can envision images of him graduating from high school, college, and then becoming a success. She imagines him getting married and having children of his own. She sees all of these things even before he has been born. How is that possible?

It is possible because she has conceived those images deep within her spirit. Not only has she conceived the seed of a child in her womb that she will one day give birth to. But she has also conceived within her the dreams, the plans, and purposes that she believes are best for that child. God has done the same with us. Jeremiah 1:5 (NLT) tells us, "I knew you before I formed you in your mother's womb. Before you were born I set you apart and appointed you as my prophet to the nations." In Jeremiah 29:11 (NIV) God says to us, "For I know the plans I have for you," declares the Lord, "plans to prosper you and not to harm you, plans to give you hope and a future."

Even before her child is born the mother begins to imagine just how she should create the baby's room. She picks out colors, a crib, toys, clothes in anticipation of his birth. She makes the necessary preparation for giving birth to that child. Faith works the same way. Once we have gone to the Word of God and found out what God has to say about us, we then begin to meditate on those truths. It is through our meditation on His Word that we begin to become pregnant with those images in our spirit. We begin to see ourselves the way that God has seen us, and nothing can move us away from our new image of who we are in Him.

For example, because we know that it is God's will for us to be healed, we begin to picture giving birth to our healing. We begin to speak the Word of God—His Precious healing Scriptures over ourselves. Then we begin to see ourselves doing the things that we couldn't do before. Once these two things (seeing and saying), have taken root in our spirit, we're well on our way to giving birth to, and living in that reality.

A word of caution at this point: don't allow the enemy, friends, or family, to paint a different picture in your spirit. Let the Word of God be your standard of TRUTH. Don't allow people who don't have the faith to believe with you, cause you to abort your dreams. In many cases it is better to keep these things to yourself until it's time to give birth to them in this world. Be careful who you share your dreams with; many people will become jealous when they SEE that you have more faith than they do. Don't let them steal the dream that is growing on the inside of you. Stay focused! Develop that picture on the inside of your spirit! Find Scriptural evidence for the things you are believing Him for. And speak only those things that God has already said about you and your circumstances in His Word. And finally, GET READY TO GIVE BIRTH!

Daily Declaration

I declare that I have the mind of Christ and that I see myself the way that God sees me. I am healed, prosperous, Blessed, well liked, highly favored by God and man, I have great kids, a wonderful and loving marriage, I am filled with peace, and I have an excellent career that gives me great pleasure and that I love to work at each day. I declare that I have a creative and sound mind. My imagination is filled with pictures of God's love and His plans for my future. I see those images and I receive them by faith. I declare that they will come to pass in my life in the name of Jesus. I think only on the things that are true, noble, just, pure, lovely, and of a good report, because my spirit is filled with God's Word. As Joshua 1:8 describes, God's Word never departs from my mouth. I meditate on His Word day and night that I may observe to do all that is within it. For this reason I live in the overflow of prosperity spirit, soul, and body, and I enjoy good success. I pray all of this in the mighty name of Jesus, Amen.

Day 26

Don't Wait! Use What You've Got!

"After him was Shamgar the son of Anath, who killed six hundred men of the Philistines with an ox goad; and he also delivered Israel."

Judges 3:31 (NKJV)

A good place to start today is by explaining that an ox goad is a staff with a sharp pointed end that was used by farmers to prod their stubborn or lazy animals while they were plowing the fields. You may be asking, "Mike, why do I care about an ox goad, I'm not a farmer?" I understand, but I want to share something that I believe you might find interesting.

Shamgar was one of the judges that God raised up after the death of Joshua, to lead the morally depraved Israelites back into relationship with Him and to lead them into victory over their enemies. After Joshua's death, the Israelites continually turned away from the true God of Israel and turned to their false gods and idols. As a result of their unfaithfulness, the Israelites were repeatedly defeated by their enemies and placed under the rule of foreign nations.

Judges 2:11-19 tells us, "[11] Then the children of Israel did evil in the sight of the Lord, and served the Baals; [12] and they forsook the Lord God of their fathers, who had brought them out of the land of

Egypt; and they followed other gods from among the gods of the people who were all around them, and they bowed down to them; and they provoked the Lord to anger. [13] They forsook the Lord and served Baal and the Ashtoreths. [14] And the anger of the Lord was hot against Israel. So He delivered them into the hands of plunderers who despoiled them; and He sold them into the hands of their enemies all around, so that they could no longer stand before their enemies. [15] Wherever they went out, the hand of the Lord was against them for calamity, as the Lord had said, and as the Lord had sworn to them. And they were greatly distressed. [16] Nevertheless, the Lord raised up judges who delivered them out of the hand of those who plundered them. [17] Yet they would not listen to their judges, but they played the harlot with other gods, and bowed down to them. They turned quickly from the way in which their fathers walked, in obeying the commandments of the Lord; they did not do so. [18] And when the Lord raised up judges for them, the Lord was with the judge and delivered them out of the hand of their enemies all the days of the judge; for the Lord was moved to pity by their groaning because of those who oppressed them and harassed them. [19] And it came to pass, when the judge was dead, that they reverted and behaved more corruptly than their fathers, by following other gods, to serve them and bow down to them. They did not cease from their own doings nor from their stubborn way."

The interesting thing is that Shamgar was used by God to get the Israelites back on track and to turn back to Him from their unfaithful ways. He single handedly killed 600 Philistines with an ox goad, a farmer's implement, used to prod stubborn oxen that would not perform as they should. Shamgar wasn't known as being a great warrior, but he was known as a farmer who obeyed and honored God. He was tired of seeing his people being perverted by the Philistines gods. He was tired of their rebellious spirit towards their Creator. He couldn't take it any longer so he decided to stand up and use the only thing that he had. He wasn't a warrior so he didn't have a sword. He wasn't a blacksmith so he didn't use a hammer. No, Shamgar was a farmer, so he used the tool that he was most familiar with while working in the fields with his oxen—an ox goad. And in doing so, he defeated the enemy armies and led his nation back to serving the Lord.

The story of Shamgar reminds me of the story of David, a teenage boy who lived out in the field with his sheep. His father and brothers saw him as an outcast, but God eventually took him from the fields tending sheep into the palace ruling the nation of Israel. It was David who defeated Goliath—the giant warrior in the Philistine army. During a time when the Israelites were again at war with the Philistines.

In 1 Samuel 17:38-41 we read, "[38] So Saul clothed David with his armor, and he put a bronze helmet on his head; he also clothed him with a coat of mail. [39] David fastened his sword to his armor and tried to walk, for he had not tested them. And David said to Saul, "I cannot walk with these, for I have not tested them." So David took them off. [40] Then he took his staff in his hand; and he chose for himself five smooth stones from the brook, and put them in a shepherd's bag, in a pouch which he had, and his sling was in his hand. And he drew near to the Philistine." Instead of trying to be somebody he wasn't, David stuck with what he was familiar with. He trusted in God and he trusted in the talents that God had deposited and refined within him while protecting his sheep. He didn't try to look or act like Saul or any of the other soldiers in Saul's army—and it's a good thing he didn't—or it would have gotten him killed.

Just like David, Shamgar trusted in God and he trusted in the ox goad that he had become familiar with. He started his battle against the Philistine army with what he already had and with the talents that he already possessed. He didn't wait for the "right time" or for "better conditions." He was tired of seeing the Israelites compromises, and he was fed-up with them bowing their knees to false gods. Shamgar was a man who esteemed the things that God values. As a result of his convictions, he succeeded by standing up and fighting for what he believed in. And he did it with the only thing he possessed—an ox goad.

Shamgar's story is also similar to a story we read about Samson, who slayed a thousand Philistines with the jawbone of a donkey. "15 He found a fresh jawbone of a donkey, reached out his hand and took it, and killed a thousand men with it. 16 Then Samson said: "With the jawbone of a donkey, heaps upon heaps, with the jawbone of a donkey I have slain a thousand men!" (See Judges 15:15-16).

Judges 3:31 and Judges 5:6 are the only two references in the Bible that mention anything about Shamgar. "In the days of Shamgar, son of Anath, in the days of Jael, the highways were deserted, and the travelers walked along the byways." (Judges 5:6). Not much for a champion of God, but we know enough about him to know that he was a man of valor and a man who was sold out for God.

Some Scholars believe that Shamgar and another man named Shammah, who is found in 2 Samuel 23:11 are the same person. "8 These are the names of the mighty men whom David had: Josheb-Basshebeth the Tachmonite, chief among the captains. He was called Adino the Eznite, because he had killed eight hundred men at one time. 9 And after him was Eleazar the son of Dodo, the Ahohite, one of the three mighty men with David when they defied the Philistines who were gathered there for battle, and the men of Israel had retreated. 10 He arose and attacked the Philistines until his hand was weary, and his hand stuck to the sword. The Lord brought about a great victory that day; and the people returned after him only to plunder. 11 *And after him was Shammah the son of Agee the Hararite. The Philistines had gathered together into a troop where there was a piece of ground full of lentils. So the people fled from the Philistines. [12] But he stationed himself in the middle of the field, defended it, and killed the Philistines. So the Lord brought about a great victory."* (2 Samuel 23:8-12).

Regardless, the truth remains that all of these great men of faith, believed in God. They made use of what they had available to them, and they fought to free their nation from demonic oppression. Each one of these people overcame "impossible circumstances," when they refused to compromise and follow the status quo. But it took courage and a willingness to fight for what they believed in. I encourage each of you to do the same thing. There's never a "perfect time" to stand up for what you believe, it's always the "right time" to stand up for what you believe! I dare you to use what you have available to you right now. I double-dog dare you to trust God, and to make a difference in this world by starting where you are right now. You probably aren't a warrior, but neither was Shamgar. He was just a simple farmer who seized the opportunity that God presented to him, and he delivered the entire nation of Israel from the oppression of the Philistines. What are you going to do? What great things are we going to be hearing and reading about you? Start where you are today! Use what you have, and do what you can, for the glory of God!

Daily Declaration

I declare that I am filled with holy boldness and the determination to make God famous in the earth. God has equipped me with everything that I need to get any and every job done that He has called me to do. I declare that I have the courage of Shamgar, the favor of David, the strength of Samson, and the mind of Christ! I can do all things in Christ Jesus who strengthens me! I am an overcomer! I am Blessed in all that I do! I am a doer of the Word of God and I have the heart to lead everyone that I meet into the saving knowledge of Jesus. Lord, use me as a vessel to bring you honor. Father, lead me to those who need to hear about Your goodness. Give me Your words and help me to speak life into their spirit. I declare that fear has no power over me. I will not cower when my enemies surround me and plot to kill me. No, I will use those things that You have given to me. I will use the tools that I have become familiar with to disarm them and either lead them to Your throne of Grace or to their destruction—it is their choice. I will use Your Word, the name of Jesus, the Blood of Jesus, and the armor of God. Just like Shamgar, these are my tools that will enable me to walk in Victory and to overcome the Devil in every battle. I pray all these things in the mighty name of Jesus, Amen.

Day 27

It Is Always A Resounding YES With God

"^{19} For the Son of God, Jesus Christ, who was preached among you by us—by me, Silvanus, and Timothy—was not Yes and No, but in Him was Yes. ^{20} For all the promises of God in Him are Yes, and in Him Amen, to the glory of God through us."

2 Corinthians 1:19-20 (NKJV)

Have you ever heard someone say, "God sometimes says yes, sometimes says no, and sometimes says wait." REALLY? Show me that from the Scripture! If your request or petition is based on the promises of the Word, God's answer is ALWAYS a definite YES!

People continually base their faith on their personal experience instead of basing it on what the Bible actually says. I have heard people say things like, "Well I asked God to heal my Aunt Minnie, and He didn't answer my prayer, she died." Was she a Believer? Then she is experiencing perfect healing in heaven right now. You and I don't know what Aunt Minnie was believing for. She may have started off believing God for her healing and then decided that she had lived a full life and was ready to go home. She may have been in excruciating pain, tired of fighting disease, and may have just decided that she was ready to leave this world. That doesn't mean that she didn't have faith, it just means that she was done fighting for her faith here. We've got to remember that just because we don't always SEE the results of the things we are praying for in this life, it doesn't change the truth of the Bible. The Word of God is clear—God's Word won't return void.

We must decide for ourselves that the BIBLE is FINAL AUTHORITY for our lives. God has commanded us to live by faith (See Habakkuk 2-2-4; Romans 1:17; Galatians 3:11; Hebrews 10:38). We don't know all of the circumstances surrounding those that we pray for. Just like with Aunt Minnie, our faith will not override the faith of the person dealing with the sickness, financial issue, broken relationship, etc. If they decide to give up and go home to be with Jesus, or if they allow doubt and unbelief to creep in and steal their confidence, then we cannot make them receive anything. God will honor their free-will decision. Remember what Job 22:28 says tells us, "You shall also decide and decree a thing, and it shall be established for you..." If Aunt Minnie was saying, "Lord, I'm ready to go home, I'm tired of fighting this disease," Her words are going to establish what happens in her life. Our prayers to keep her here aren't going to cancel out her decision to be released from her pain. She has made the choice to go home to her Savior.

Another truth that many people don't understand is that our words have power. What we say matters. We cannot say one thing and then contradict it with the opposite, and still expect God to honor our requests for healing or anything else. E.W. Kenyon once said, "Your words are either life-producing or death-dealing, because when you choose to agree with God by speaking His Word, He walks with you in every area of your life. Jesus is Lord of our affirmations. He is the

Author and Finisher of our faith. He is the High Priest of our confession."

Don Gossett writes, "If we speak only what our senses dictate, we will not be agreeing with God. It is through speaking the Word that we agree with God. It is the confession of faith that is our victory. To walk with God, we must disagree with the devil, as Jesus did, by boldly declaring, 'it is written...'"

James 1:5-8 tells us that we must not be double minded if we are to expect anything from God. It is imperative that we ask of God believing to receive what we have prayed and then stand confident in our faith until we receive what we have asked, regardless of what our five physical senses are telling us. If we begin confessing healing and then start speaking doubt and unbelief based on what we "feel," we are being double minded. As a result, The Bible says that we can expect to receive nothing!

Remember James 1:17 "Every good gift and every perfect gift is from above, and comes down from the Father of lights, with whom there is no variation or shadow of turning." Everything good is from God. God is a Good God and He wants us blessed. He wants us to receive the answers to our prayers. But if we want to experience and enjoy the requests that we have asked of Him, we've got to remain confident and steadfast in our faith for those things, until they manifest.

Real Bible faith operates this way: it remains focused on God's Word as FINAL AUTHORITY, casting down imaginations and conflicting images that the devil tries to convince us to receive. (See 2 Corinthians 10:5). Faith speaks the Word of God ONLY!

Every time the devil tries to tell you that you can't have that thing that God has promised you, shout in his face and tell him that he's a liar! Remind him that your Heavenly Father has already told you that you already have what was promised to you IN JESUS. Remind him that you are a person of the Word, and that it is written! "For all the promises of God in Him are YES, and in Him AMEN, to the glory of God!" Hallelujah! God is for you and His promise to you is YES! God has said it, we believe it, and that settles it! Amen!

Daily Declaration

I declare that God's promises are ALWAYS Yes and Amen in my life. If God has said it, I have it now, in the name of Jesus. I declare that the Bible is the standard for my life. I know that God's Word will not return to me void. Just as God spoke His Word and received what He said, I speak His Word and I receive what I say. Father, I thank you for giving me all things which pertain to life and godliness (See 2 Peter 1:3). I receive everything that I pray for when I pray. I bind doubt and I forbid it to try to hinder me in any way. I am steadfast in my faith. I refuse to be double-minded. I declare that I am a joint-heir with Christ. I have inherited THE BLESSING and I walk in God's favor each and every day. I am surrounded by His goodness, His mercy, and His perfect peace. I speak peace to my body, peace to my finances, peace to my mind and emotions, and peace to my family. Jesus said in John 14:27, "Peace [wholeness], I leave with you, My peace [total life Blessing], I give to you; not as the world gives do I give to you. Let not your heart be troubled, neither let it be afraid." I believe that Jesus meant what He said and that He said what He meant. I receive all of His promises right now, by faith, in Jesus' name, Amen.

Day 28

Persistence Breaks Resistance

"When there was nothing left to hope for, Abraham still hoped and believed. As a result, he became a father of many nations, as he had been told: "That is how many descendants you will have."

Romans 4:18 (God's Word Translation)

Have you ever noticed that those people, who continue to press forward toward their goals even when they have failed in the past, tend to become the most successful people in the world?

Winston Churchill the twice elected Prime Minister of Brittan, failed sixth grade and was defeated in every political race he ever participated in, until the age of 62, when he won the election for Prime Minister. He later won the Nobel Peace Prize and is known worldwide as a great thinker, a man of enormous courage, and an unparalleled historic figure.

Thomas Edison was told by his teachers as a young boy, that he was too stupid to ever amount to anything. As an adult, Edison was fired from his first two careers and told that it was because he was unproductive. He later became a prolific inventor of such things as the light bulb, phonograph, and telegraph, just to name a few. But it took Edison over 1000 attempts to perfect a light bulb design that worked.

Charles Shultz the renowned artist of the Peanuts gang featuring Snoopy, Woodstock, Charlie Brown, and Lucy had every one of the cartoons that he submitted to his high school yearbook rejected. As a young adult, Schultz tried to get a job working for Walt Disney, but was rejected there too. But Shultz fought his way to the top. His tenacity, hard work, and believe-that-you-can attitude propelled him to become a mogul in the cartoon industry. His name and his characters are loved around the world and were until his death, featured in weekly in many newspapers nationally.

J.K. Rowling who became famous for her Harry Potter novels, was penniless and on welfare. She was divorced and raising a child, all the while attending school and writing a novel. Within a period of five years, she went from welfare to becoming one of the richest women in the world.

Michael Jordan known as probably the most talented basketball player of all time was cut from his high school basketball team, but he didn't let that stop him from playing the game he loved. He has been quoted for saying that he has missed over 9000 shots in his career and lost over 300 games, but that even through all of his failure, his tenacity to keep playing the game, and his burning desire to become better is what has made him a success.

In the Bible we find people with the Spirit of Faith and determination to move forward at all costs. People such as Abraham who spent over 20 years believing God for his promised heir, and Noah who spent 100 years building an ark, even though he had never even seen rain. What about David who was anointed king of Israel, but spent years running from King Saul and even his own son who sought to kill him. Or Joseph who had been given a vision by God, yet he endured slavery, imprisonment, and hard times before ever seeing a glimpse of that promise in the natural.

I am also reminded of the woman with the issue of blood, found in Mark chapter 5. The Bible says, "[25] In the crowd was a woman who had been suffering from chronic bleeding for twelve years. [26] Although she had been under the care of many doctors and had spent all her money, she had not been helped at all. Actually, she had become worse." (Mark 5:25-26, GWT).

This woman spent 12 years suffering from that horrible disease. She spent all of the money she owned trying to be healed by physicians, but had no success. In verses 27-28, we read that she heard Jesus was in town and she believed that if she could just touch the hem of His garment, that she would be healed and made whole. Even though every doctor had failed to cure her disease, this woman still persisted in her faith, believing that she could receive her healing. She understood because she was considered to be unclean according to Jewish law, that she could be stoned for mingling amongst people in the crowd. But she would not allow that fear to stop her! And as her reward, Jesus says to her, "Daughter, your faith has made you well. Go in peace! Be cured from your illness." (Mark 5:34, GWT).

It was persistence, tenacity, and the Spirit of Faith that brought all of these people from a place of bondage and lack into their place of triumph and victory. Sure, not all of the people mentioned were professing Christians, but the laws of faith do not discriminate who they will work for and who they won't. Just like the law of gravity demands that anything that is thrown up must come down, the law of faith and persistence always leads to breakthrough for the person who refuses to doubt and continues to believe God by receiving and acting on His promises.

If you will determine to remain persistent and continue to believe for God's best for your life—you too, will eventually be living your dreams. Don't quit! Continue fighting for your dreams and desires through continued persistence and faith and you will overcome every obstacle and all of the resistance that is trying to keep you from achieving your victory in Jesus. Persistence will break the bonds of resistance in your life!

Daily Declaration

I declare that I am persistent and steadfast in my faith. I refuse to let go of God's promises for my life. Jesus has given me the victory and has made me an overcomer in Him. There is nothing that is impossible for me, because Jesus has promised that nothing is impossible to him who believes (See Mark 9:23). I am a believer and not a doubter. I believe that God's Word will not return to me void, just as it won't return void to God. God's Word spoken out of my mouth is just as powerful as God's Word spoken out of His mouth. My Heavenly Father has created me in His image and likeness. I am a faith-filled spirit man/woman who has been given the authority to declare God's promises and to receive everything that I have declared. I decree that I live in the Blessing of God and I walk in continual Victory in Jesus. I believe that I receive everything that I have just prayed for in Jesus mighty name of Jesus, Amen.

Day 29

God's Word Spoken Out Of Your Mouth, Will Turn Your Mountains Into Molehills

"So, big mountain, who do you think you are? Next to Zerubbabel you're nothing but a molehill. He'll proceed to set the Cornerstone in place, accompanied by cheers: Yes! Yes! Do it!"

Zechariah 4:7 (MSG)

Many people, when faced with obstacles, tend to talk about their problems. They talk to anyone who is willing to listen to them. They talk about how hard their life is because of what they are facing. They talk about how impossible their circumstances look and feel, or about how much pain they are currently experiencing. Some even use their trials as the excuse for not attaining their life goals. But each of us knows in our heart that even though our obstacles are difficult, we can overcome them all in Jesus—Who has overcome them for us already.

Jesus told us in John 16:33, "These things I have spoken to you, that in Me you may have peace. In the world you will have tribulation; but be of good cheer, I have overcome the world." In 1 John 4:4 we are told, "You are of God, little children, and have overcome them, because He who is in you is greater than he who is in the world."

I understand that many of the obstacles that we face are challenging and even life threatening in some cases, but talking about how big the problem is does absolutely nothing to get it out of our way. In fact, all talking about the problem does for us is to magnify its power in our life, and help us to feel defeated and powerless against it. That is exactly what the twelve spies did when they were sent into the Promised Land to spy on the people that were living there. They saw all of the amazing opportunity that lay before them, but brushed it off because of their stinkin' thinking, and fear.

When the spies gave their report they said to the congregation, "The land through which we have gone as spies is a land that devours its inhabitants, and all the people whom we saw in it are men of great stature. [33] There we saw the giants (the descendants of Anak came from the giants); and we were like grasshoppers in our own sight, and so we were in their sight." Instead of focusing on the bounty available to them, the fertile soil, and all of the other amazing opportunities, they focused on the one negative that stood between them and the promise of God—the size of the people. They had one hundred positive things to rejoice about and only one negative, and yet God even promised to make them victorious over their enemies. Amazing!

A young man that I know struggles with this same kind of unbelief and negativity. I have been praying and working with him for about two years. He has spent the entire time I've known him on government support while finishing school and looking for a career that will pay him a good salary. Finally, two months ago he was hired by a temp agency to work for a huge corporation. Because he has done so well in that position the corporation hired him on full-time and gave him a large salary increase. He went from making about $12.00 per hour to making $45K per year, with full benefits.

My friend was ecstatic for about an hour or two, telling me about all of the benefits his new position was going to make available to him. He told me that the company had informed him that they were prepping him to lead his department. But immediately after telling me about all of the benefits he'd just received, all he could focus on was how much his taxes would be. Even after taxes he would still be making about $20K more per year than he was on government support. I was amazed by his negativity. He would finally have the medical and dental insurance that he had been praying for. He would finally be able to start saving for retirement in his new 401K plan. He was finally moving into the real world and beginning his first "real" job, but all he could think about was the negative aspect of having to pay taxes just like every other able bodied, human being in America. It truly made me sad to see how unappreciative most people are towards the Blessing of God. I felt like telling him, "Welcome to the real world Junior, get over it and rejoice in your promotion!"

Thomas Edison was quoted as saying, "Opportunity is missed by most people because it is dressed in overalls and looks like work." I wonder how many people miss out on the opportunities that God is placing before them either because they are too lazy to do the work to reap the benefits, or because they magnify minor obstacles that stand between them and their harvest—instead of magnifying God!

Obstacles are often disguised as mountains. They often look like huge behemoths that stand between us and our destiny. When we look at them up close, we can't see our way around them. Oftentimes, the thought of climbing over them may seem like an impossibility. We know that if we were to tunnel through our mountain, it might take us years and a lot of wasted energy. But God never told us to climb over, to go around, or to tunnel through our mountains—He told us to SPEAK TO THEM and to COMMAND THE TO MOVE OUT OF OUR WAY!

In Matthew 21:21-22 Jesus told His disciples, "²¹Assuredly, I say to you, if you have faith and do not doubt, you will not only do what was done to the fig tree, but also if you say to this mountain, 'Be removed and be cast into the sea,' it will be done. ²² And whatever things you ask in prayer, believing, you will receive."

I like what Zechariah had to say when faced with the enormous task of rebuilding the Temple in Jerusalem. The capstone is the last piece that is usually added to a structure. It signifies the completion and is also usually a beautiful decorative piece. It can also be a symbol of victory and a job well done. In Zechariah 4:7 we read what the angel of the Lord declared to Zechariah in his vision, "So, big mountain, who do you think you are? Next to Zerubbabel you're nothing but a molehill. He'll proceed to set the Cornerstone [capstone—NKJV] in place, accompanied by cheers: Yes! Yes! Do it!"

Do you see that? The angel of the Lord spoke to the mountain that stood before Zerubbabel, and reminded it that it was no match for our Great God. The angel reminded that obstacle that it must bow before the covenant child of God and submit to his/her authority. He spoke to the mountain declaring, "Look mountain—look you obstacle that is trying to stand before My people Israel, you may look impossible, you may look too big to overcome, but you are nothing more than a tiny mole hill before My people, because I AM their God. They will succeed in everything that they put their hands to, and they will sing about their victory in Me. Their songs will be heard around the world—for I Am their strength, their promise, and the One who backs every promise that I have given to them in My Word."

That is exactly the same way we must look at our obstacles, set-backs, and any circumstance that tries to discourage us from completing our God-ordained tasks or desires. There is NOTHING TOO BIG FOR OUR GOD. There is nothing that is too big for us either, because we are His children. We will receive our victory in Jesus, if we will have the courage to keep moving forward in our faith and keep speaking the Word of God over the mountains that try to stand in our way. There's no time to waste going around, going over, or trying to tunnel through our problems. No, Speak to those obstacles and command them to move out of your way in the name of Jesus!

Don't waste your time telling others about how big your challenges are. Instead, begin telling your problems how BIG YOUR GOD IS. Begin saying things like, "Look here mountain of debt, look here mountain of sickness—you are nothing more than a tiny mole hill and I have victory over you in the name of Jesus! Get out of my way, be cast into the sea, and never return to me or my family, in the name of Jesus!" Then keep moving right along as you were before that mountain appeared. God's favor spoken out of your mouth will turn your mountains into molehills. You are an overcomer and more than a conqueror in Jesus Christ, Amen!

Daily Declaration

I declare that every obstacle that is trying to stand between me and God's promises for my life is broken now. Nothing can separate me from the love of God or from His will for my life (See Romans 8:31-39). God sees me Blessed! He sees me whole and lacking no good thing (See Psalm 34:10 and Psalm 84:11). I have renewed my mind to His Word and I see myself the way that God sees me (See Romans 12:1-2). Jesus promised me in Mark 11:23-24 (NLT), "[23] I tell you the truth, you can say to this mountain, 'May you be lifted up and thrown into the sea,' and it will happen. But you must really believe it will happen and have no doubt in your heart. [24] I tell you, you can pray for anything, and if you believe that you've received it, it will be yours." The Bible says that, "The Lord will command the blessing on you in your storehouses and in all to which you set your hand, and He will bless you in the land which the Lord your God is giving you." I receive all that God has for me through my faith in Jesus. For God has said to me, "All these blessings shall come upon you and overtake you, because you obey the voice of the Lord your God." (See Deuteronomy 28:2). Moreover, God has given me the power to get wealth which includes: spiritual, physical, emotional, mental relational, material, and financial prosperity. (See Deuteronomy 8:18). I declare that all of those things are mine now in Jesus' name, Amen.

Day 30

Fear And Doubt: The Bipolar Twins

"²⁸ And Peter answered Him and said, "Lord, if it is You, command me to come to You on the water." ²⁹ So He said, "Come." And when Peter had come down out of the boat, he walked on the water to go to Jesus. ³⁰ But when he saw that the wind was boisterous, he was afraid; and beginning to sink he cried out, saying, "Lord, save me!" And immediately Jesus stretched out His hand and caught him, and said to him, "O you of little faith, why did you doubt?"

Matthew 14:28-31 (NKJV)

How many times have you set out to do something big in your life or in the lives of another, when all of a sudden fear and doubt came knocking on your door? Then when you came to the door to see who was there, fear jumped out at you and began shouting lies in your face. Fears claiming that you are either too old or too young to accomplish what you had planned. Fears telling you that you don't have the experience you need to get the job done. Or the fears that tell you that if you follow through and Bless that person that God has instructed you to Bless, that you won't have enough left over to take care of yourself.

I struggled with similar fears like these for a long time. I had feelings of inadequacy. I believed that I wasn't good enough, smart enough, or talented enough to be a minister. I compared myself to my heroes and came up short every time. There were a myriad of reasons why I should have given up and started looking for another profession. But I just couldn't get free from the knowledge that I wasn't the one who chose this life for myself. In fact, ministry was the furthest thing from my plans for my life. I knew that God was the One who had both called me and gifted me with the ability to be a minister of His Gospel. The Bible says, "[29]God's gifts and God's call are under full warranty—never canceled, never rescinded. [30-32] There was a time not so long ago when you were on the outs with God. But then the Jews slammed the door on him and things opened up for you. Now they are on the outs. But with the door held wide open for you, they have a way back in. In one way or another, God makes sure that we all experience what it means to be outside so that he can personally open the door and welcome us back in." (See Romans 11:29-32). Thank God for His mercy and grace. Thank God for our Jewish brothers and sisters. God has promised that they will all be saved too, because they are His chosen people. Hallelujah! Thank You Jesus for Your faithfulness!

I know that I am not alone in my negative thinking. I know that we all face areas in our lives where we have insecurities and feel inadequate, but as the old saying goes: practice makes perfect. Or maybe I should say, practice: continuing to do what God has called us to do, and our faith in His ability work through us, will open up doors on the inside of our spirit that will pull the anointing out of us and help us get the job done right—no matter where we lack in personal our ability or talent.

We must realize that both fear and doubt have multiple personalities; they are in a sense bipolar. One minute they tell us things like, "You can't do that, it's impossible." Or it tells us things like, "You can ONLY do it if you do it all at once." Or maybe something like, "You can have that thing that you are believing for, if you sacrifice that other thing that you want." Well which one is it? That's just it—Fear is a lie! Fear NEVER MAKES SENSE! If we thought about what fear and doubt were telling us from a rational perspective—we'd understand that those tactics are meant only to cause confusion and to turn us away from faith.

Each time fear or doubt come your way, I want you to do something that will throw these bipolar twins off guard. When fear and doubt come to you telling you why you can't accomplish something, tell them that you have learned to doubt your doubts, and say, "I doubt that." When fear tries to tell you that something is impossible, shout back, "I doubt that, the Bible says nothing is impossible to him who believes, and I am a Believer. Believing is what I do." (See Mark 9:23). When doubt screams, "But you're too young or you're too old to accomplish that..." Scream back, "I doubt that—I can do all things through Christ who strengthens me." (See Philippians 4:13). Every time fear and doubt try to distract you from accomplishing your mission, remind them what the Word of God has to say about it—Tell them, "It is written..." and then remember that you don't have to accomplish it in your own power—but that you will accomplish it in the power and ability of Christ in you, the hope of glory.

Colossians 1:25-27 tells us, "I became a minister according to the stewardship from God which was given to me for you, to fulfill the word of God, [26] the mystery which has been hidden from ages and from generations, but now has been revealed to His saints. [27] To them

God willed to make known what are the riches of the glory of this mystery among the Gentiles: **which is Christ in you, the hope of glory.**" (Emphasis Added).

What does this mean to us? It means that God is the One who has called you to be His spokesperson. He is the One who has called you to be His Ambassadors in the earth, and to accomplish His will for your life. If you are His child, He has placed inside of you everything you need to get your job done correctly. He has not only given you the ability, but He has deposited Himself inside of you—Christ in you the hope of glory. You have Jesus, the anointed Messiah, and The Way Maker, alive and working inside of you to fully accomplish the task at hand. Jesus is the Glory of God; He is the Light, and the Power, Who will bring you good success, when you do what you've been called to do.

Many people think Peter failed when he attempted to walk on the water, but he didn't. Peter asked Jesus, Lord, if that is You; command me to come to you on the water. And Jesus said—COME. Peter had the amazing courage to step out of the boat and to take that first step on the water. He might not have made it a mile, he might not have made it a block, but he made it further than any other person who has ever lived, excluding Jesus—and that is SUCCESS! It was only when he began to listen to fear and doubt that he began to sink.

Don't listen to the voices of fear and doubt. Don't pay attention to self-criticism, insecurities, or anything other than the voice of God. If God has called you to do something, then He will give you the ability to get it done right. You weren't necessarily created to do it the same way anyone else would do it; otherwise God would have used the other people to get the job done. Recognize that you may make mistakes here and there, but mistakes are just part of learning and growing up in Him. If you will seek God and obey His voice, you will cross the finish line a CHAMPION. Refuse to listen to fear and doubt—after all, one minute they will tell you one thing, and the next they tell you exactly the opposite. Steer clear of the bi-polar twins by rebuking them in the name of Jesus and then by speaking the Word and building yourself up in your most holy faith (See Jude 1:20). God is good all the time!

Daily Declaration

I declare that fear and doubt have no authority in my life. I refuse to doubt because I am a Believer. And I refuse to fear, because God has not given me the spirit of fear, but of power and of love and of a sound mind. (See 2 Timothy 1:7). I have the mind of Christ, and fear is far from me. I walk in the love of God and my faith is working to produce everything that I believe and speak (See Galatians 5:6). When the Pharisee asked Jesus which was the greatest commandment in the Bible, "[37] Jesus said to him, "'You shall love the Lord your God with all your heart, with all your soul, and with all your mind.'[38] This is the first and great commandment. [39] And the second is like it: 'You shall love your neighbor as yourself.' [40] On these two commandments hang all the Law and the Prophets." I declare that because I continually operate in love, I am Blessed in all that I do. 1 Corinthians 13:13 (NLT) tells me, "Three things will last forever—faith, hope, and love—and the greatest of these is love." Because I am proficient in all of these, I will have no problem receiving all that God has for me. Fear and doubt are no match against my spiritual weapons of faith, hope, and love. Each of these is alive in me, around me, and working through me to produce God's best in my life. I call myself Blessed in Jesus' name, Amen.

Day 31

From Nothing, To The Land Of More Than Enough!

"They will not be disgraced in hard times; even in famine they will have more than enough."

Psalm 37:19 (NLT)

Since 2008 many people have experienced a myriad of difficulties and downturns. Some have lost jobs, lost their homes, lost their nest eggs. Many who were ready to retire have had to start all over in new careers just to survive. But no matter what we have had to endure, God has made us a promise that we can take to heart. Psalm 37:19 (NLT) tells us, "They will not be disgraced in hard times; even in famine they will have more than enough." God's promised that we will have more than enough even during the most difficult seasons of life—and we can believe Him.

I know how many of you may be feeling if you have experienced trials like these. I too have faced some difficult situations and circumstances over the last few years. We may not have gone through the same things—but tough times are tough times. Even though the trials we face may seem excruciating while we are going through them, we must not allow our focus to remain on the negative aspects that we are experiencing. Our eyes need to move from our current pressures and refocus on the promises of God and the hope we have in Him. I'm not just talking about our future in Heaven, but I'm also talking about the promises that He has given to us while we are here in the earth. God has promised to care for us and to be our Source in ALL THINGS!

Look at the promise that we have in Psalm 37:23-26, "The steps of a good man are ordered by the Lord, and He delights in his way. [24] Though he fall, he shall not be utterly cast down; for the Lord upholds him with His hand. [25] I have been young, and now am old; yet I have not seen the righteous forsaken, nor his descendants begging bread. [26] He is ever merciful, and lends; and his descendants are blessed." We can take this promise to the bank. God is our Source, our Protector, and our faithful covenant keeping God.

One of my favorite promises is found in Psalm 37:19 which says, "…even in famine they will have more than enough." That is something to shout about! You may not be exactly where you want to be financially right this minute. There are probably many things that you wish you could be doing if you only had a little more money. Maybe you'd buy a newer car, maybe you'd go on a vacation, or maybe you'd just like to buy a few new clothes—I understand—really I do! But the way we get to that place of MORE THAN ENOUGH is by rejoicing and thanking God for all that He has already done for us.

He has provided everything up to now. He has been faithful to pay all of your bills. He has provided food for you to eat. He has kept your car running perfectly even though it should have died years ago. And He has even made your older clothes last and look good—those are all Blessings of God. Begin praising Him where you are now and soon you'll be praising Him for the new things He's bringing your way. Our God is a faithful God and He won't forsake you or leave you alone and without the support of the things you need or desire.

The Message Bible renders Psalm 37:19 the following way: "In hard times, they'll hold their heads high; when the shelves are bare, they'll be full." Rejoice in the fact that you are not starving, that your belly is full, and that you are in much better shape than many other people. I am not trying to make light of what you have gone through, but I want you to understand that without God it would have been much worse.

I know that hard times can wear on your mind and on your soul, but I want you to understand and to look at the bigger picture. Where would you be if it had not been for the Lord? Even though you may not be where you think you are supposed to be, even though you thought you'd be much further along than you are right now—you are still very Blessed indeed! There are some people who have lost everything. You've only endured a *TEMPORARY* set-back! If you are a person of faith you're not planning on camping out in the valley of drought, lack, and not enough—but you're believing God to bring you out and bring you up.

In Psalm 23:4-6 David writes, "[4] Yea, though I walk through the valley of the shadow of death, I will fear no evil; for You are with me; Your rod and Your staff, they comfort me. [5] You prepare a table before me in the presence of my enemies; You anoint my head with oil; My cup runs over. [6] Surely goodness and mercy shall follow me all the days of my life; and I will dwell in the house of the Lord forever." I love David's attitude and His ability to see the goodness of God even in the midst of turmoil.

Begin to find ways to focus on God's goodness and His mercy in the Blessings He has already provided for you. Don't get stuck looking at all of the things you don't have, but begin to count your

Blessings. You have been created to be a world overcomer! God is faithful and He will bring you out of *lo debar* (the place of nothing) into your Promised Land (your place of more than enough). Come to the understanding that no matter where you may be now is not the place that you will finish. Continue to thank God for your increase, your promotion, and your victory—and He will take you there sooner than you can imagine.

1 Corinthians 10:13 declares, "No temptation has overtaken you except such as is common to man; but God is faithful, who will not allow you to be tempted beyond what you are able, ***but with the temptation will also make the way of escape***, that you may be able to bear it." (Emphasis Added). God has your escape plan already mapped out if you will just keep pressing forward in faith. It may feel as if you are walking through the Valley of the Shadow of Death, but keep walking, don't stop and camp out there, that's no place to live. You need to remember that God hasn't taken you through that place to teach you a lesson, but you're there because there is a real devil who is hell-bent on stealing, killing, and destroying everything in your life.

I love what we read in 2 Samuel 9:1-9. It is a picture of God's faithfulness to His covenant children. In this passage King David, who had made a covenant with Jonathan, Saul's son, shows mercy towards Jonathan's crippled son Mephibosheth, who is living in the town of *lo debar*, the place of nothing, of lack, and not enough.

"[1] Now David said, "Is there still anyone who is left of the house of Saul, that I may show him kindness for Jonathan's sake?" [2] And there was a servant of the house of Saul whose name was Ziba. So when they had called him to David, the king said to him, "Are you Ziba?" He said, "At your service!" [3] Then the king said, "Is there not still someone of the house of Saul, to whom I may show the kindness of God?" And Ziba said to the king, "There is still a son of Jonathan

MICHAEL VIDAURRI, D. MIN.

who is lame in his feet." [4] So the king said to him, "Where is he?" And Ziba said to the king, "Indeed he is in the house of Machir the son of Ammiel, in **Lo Debar.**" [5] Then King David sent and brought him out of the house of Machir the son of Ammiel, from Lo Debar. [6] Now when Mephibosheth the son of Jonathan, the son of Saul, had come to David, he fell on his face and prostrated himself. Then David said, "Mephibosheth?" And he answered, "Here is your servant!" [7] So David said to him, *"Do not fear, for I will surely show you kindness for Jonathan your father's sake, and will restore to you all the land of Saul your grandfather; and you shall eat bread at my table continually."* [8] Then he bowed himself, and said, "What is your servant, that you should look upon such a dead dog as I?" [9] And the king called to Ziba, Saul's servant, and said to him, "I have given to your master's son all that belonged to Saul and to all his house." (Emphasis Added).

Think about this for just a minute. David has been running from King Saul for years. Saul was jealous and on a mission to kill David. Yet because of David's covenant relationship with Jonathan, he restores Mephibosheth to the place of wealth and more than enough. If a man can act in such a merciful and faithful way then how much more will God do this for us?

Even though you may be feeling like you have been living in *lo debar*, don't become ungrateful for what you do have. You have your health; you have your family, you have many things that you can still be thankful for. Don't discount the Blessing that you do have and begin to complain or grumble. God hasn't put you where you are, but He can take you out and take you up. Keep trusting Him. Keep speaking the Blessing over yourself and all of your circumstances. Speak and believe your way into your Promised Land—it won't be long if you don't give up! In fact, I believe that you're on your way out of *lo debar* right now. Will you agree and add your faith with mine? Agree with me today, and allow God to take you from a place of nothing (*Lo Debar*) into your place of More Than Enough. This is my prayer for you today, in the mighty name of Jesus!!! Amen.

Daily Declaration

I declare that I am coming out of *Lo Debar*, and that I am coming up to the place of More Than Enough, in the name of Jesus. It is God's will for me to live in His Blessing. God has commanded His Blessing on me. He said that His Blessing will find me and overtake me. I receive those promises for my life, for my family, for my business, and for my finances, in the name of Jesus. He has Blessed me so that I can be a Blessing to others. Father, I promise to find ways to Bless other people who are in need because You have been so good to me. I want to share Your goodness with others so they see You for who You are. I declare that my days of living in lack, not enough, sickness, and the Curse are over! I have been redeemed from the Curse by my Savior, Jesus. Heavenly Father You have delivered me out of darkness and into His marvelous light (See 1 Peter 2:9). Thank you for making me a child of the light. Thank you for rescuing me out from the Curse and for taking me into Your grace, Your mercy, and into Your total life prosperity and abundance In Jesus! I pray all of this in Jesus' name, Amen.

Made in the USA
Monee, IL
16 November 2021